Praying Through the Tough Times

LLOYD JOHN OGILVIE

HARVEST HOUSE PUBLISHERS

EUGENE, OREGON

Cover by Koechel Peterson & Associates, Inc., Minneapolis, Minnesota

Cover photo © Stockxpert / Jupiterimages Unlimited

PRAYING THROUGH THE TOUGH TIMES
Abridged from original edition
Copyright © 2005 by Lloyd John Ogilvie
Published by Harvest House Publishers Eugene, Oregon 97402
www.harvesthousepublishers.com

Library of Congress Cataloging-in-Publication Data
    Ogilvie, Lloyd John.
    Praying through the tough times / Lloyd John Ogilvie. p. cm.
    ISBN 978-0-7369-2771-0 (pbk.)
    1.   Suffering—Prayer-books and devotions—English. 2. Prayers. I. Title.
    BV283.S84037 2005
    242'.86—dc22

                                                            2004019445

Printed in the United States of America

    11 12 13 14 15 16 17 18 / BP-SK / 10 9 8 7 6

CONTENTS

God Himself Is the Answer 5

When You Want to Pray...

1. In Tough Times 7

2. In Times of Grief and Pain 41

3. In Times of Problems 63

4. In Times of Trying Relationships 91

5. In Times When God Himself
   Is the Answer 111

ACKNOWLEDGMENTS

I want to express my deep gratitude to my former
assistant, Sandee Hastings, for her enthusiasm and
affirmation of this book and for her excellent and
tireless efforts in typing the manuscript for publication.

GOD HIMSELF IS THE ANSWER

Tough times. We all have them. Perhaps you are in one of those times right now.

It's often when we need God most that we find it hard to talk with Him. Our "why me's?" lead us into doubt, resentment, and finally a feeling of the absence of God. He hasn't left or changed, but we develop a low-grade agnosticism that leads to the neglect of prayer.

Then our "Lord, get me out of this!" eventually comes to "Lord, what do You want me to get out of this?" Our motto becomes "Things don't work out—God works out things!"

This book of prayers for tough times was written during my time of healing from grief after my wife of 52 years, Mary Jane, graduated to heaven. The prayers are in the first-person singular so they can be a very personal expression. They represent my own deepest thoughts and feelings, as well as those shared with me by fellow strugglers I've known and counseled through the many years of my ministry.

In all these prayers, I've tried to live in your skin and give wings to your own anguish or anxiety, or your praise and adoration. The undergirding conviction within them is, *God Himself is the Answer.* What we all need in tough times is an intimate, healing, inspiring experience of His grace and goodness, peace and power. Where I have included a Scripture quotation, the source is found at the end of the prayer to assist you in further reflection.

Prayer begins with God, and sweeps into our minds and hearts. He clarifies what He desires for us so that we can pray with boldness for what He is more ready to give than we may have been willing to ask. Prayer is the source of healing and hope in tough times.

My deepest longing is that this book will be a guide for honest, healing, and hopeful prayer for you whenever tough times come and the going is rough. God's promise to never leave or forsake us is absolutely true and reliable. I know!

Lloyd John Ogilvie

PART 1

In Tough Times

WHEN I NEED FAITH
TODAY FOR TOMORROW

Christ in you, the hope of glory.

COLOSSIANS 1:27

Christ, my Lord, indwelling, inspiring, infusing power for courageous living in tough times, remind me that You only expect from me what You have placed or will place within me. You taught me to pray for daily bread. Thank You for the revelation that means bread today for tomorrow. You will give me today what I will need tomorrow. That's amazing, Lord!

I want to learn how to pray through tough times. Help me to know that You will equip me in advance as well as during the tough times. You will take up residence in me and provide the gift of faith to be applied to the crises I may have to confront. You are the Source of it all! You endow me with primary faith to accept You as Savior and Lord and invite You to make my soul Your home…but You also empower me with faith to accomplish what will be the very best for my life. So I don't need to thrash about trying to conjure up enough faith to face tough times; rather, I can claim Your faith in me and what can be done by You for Your glory in me and around me.

As I pray through tough times You will release in me the aspect of Your character I most need for the circumstances ahead—courage, patience, endurance, discernment, wisdom, tenacity, and hope. I will be faithful because I will be full of Your gift of faith to be expressed through me. You have offered me the abounding, unsearchable riches of Your own limitless resources. Today...for tomorrow! You are my strength in tough times. Amen.

> By grace you have been saved through faith,
> and that not of yourselves; it is the gift of God.
>
> EPHESIANS 2:8

WHEN I NEED
GOD'S FAITHFULNESS

Mercy unto you, and peace, and love, be multiplied.

JUDE 2 KJV

Almighty God, it's an assurance of Your faithfulness I need in tough times. And all I need to do is turn to the Bible to hear the resounding affirmation of Your faithfulness. You told me Yourself, "My faithfulness shall be with you." Jeremiah was comforted at a very difficult time and could say, "The Lord's mercies...are new every morning; great is Your faithfulness." The psalmist couldn't express his gratitude enough: "I will sing of the mercies of the LORD forever; with my mouth will I make known Your faithfulness to all generations."

I need a character transplant from You as I face the challenges ahead today. Especially I want to be known for Your character trait of faithfulness. In spite of contradictory circumstances, I am committed to remain faithful to You, to my belief in Your goodness, and to the people who look to me for hope and inspiration for their own tough times. I pray that I may "be steadfast, immovable, always abounding in the work of the Lord," knowing that my labor "is not in vain in the Lord." You are faithful! I can make it through today with that assurance. Amen. (Psalm 89:2,4; Lamentations 3:23; Psalm 89:1; 1 Corinthians 15:58.)

He giveth more grace.

JAMES 4:6 KJV

He increaseth strength.

ISAIAH 40:29 KJV

He giveth more grace when the burdens grow greater,
    He sendeth more strength when the labors increase;
To added affliction He addeth His mercy, To multiplied trials, His multiplied peace.

When we have exhausted our store of endurance,
    When our strength has failed ere the day is half done,
When we reach the end of our hoarded resources,
Our Father's full giving is only begun.

His love has no limit, His grace has no measure, His pow'r has no boundary known unto men;
For out of His infinite riches in Jesus, He giveth, and giveth, and giveth again!

ANNIE JOHNSON FLINT

WHEN I NEED HOPE

This I recall to my mind, therefore I have hope.
Through the LORD's mercies we are not consumed,
because His compassions fail not. They are
new every morning; great is Your faithfulness.

LAMENTATIONS 3:21-23

Dear God, I need hope! I long for authentic hope that is more than shallow optimism, wishful thinking, or anxious yearning.

You are the God of hope. It is awesome to be reminded that You have been thinking about me. Even better, it is profoundly comforting to know what You think about me and my circumstances. You want me to experience peace today and bright hope for tomorrow. You stay my mind on You. Your compassion for me stirs me; Your faithfulness never fails; Your timely interventions remind me that You keep Your gracious promises.

The sure foundation of my hope is Christ's resurrection from the dead, and the strength of my hope is in His presence and power. Today I intentionally commit all my concerns to You. This commitment is like a diminutive death to my tenacious tight grip of control.

My sure hope now is for a resurrection to new life in my soul and miraculous resolution of those heart-aching worries. As You raised Jesus from the dead, You raise me out of the graves of discouragement. You fill me with a living hope that no trouble can destroy, no fear can disturb. I'm alive forever, and I'm going to live this day to the fullest.

Now focus my attention on people in my life who need hope. Make me a communicator of Your hope. Hope through me, God of hope!

Hope through me, God of Hope
Or never can I know
Deep wells of living streams of hope,
And pools of overflow.
O blessed Hope of God
Flow through me patiently,
Until I hope for everyone
As You have hoped for me.

AMY CARMICHAEL

WHEN I EXPECT TOO LITTLE

Blessed Lord Jesus, thank You for the gifts of life, intellect, good memories, and daring dreams. I don't ask for challenges equal to my talent and training, education and experience; rather, I ask for opportunities equal to Your power and vision. Forgive me when I pare life down to what I could do on my own without Your power. Make me an adventuresome, undaunted person who seeks to know what You want done and attempts it because You will provide me with exactly what I will need to accomplish it. I thank You that tough times are nothing more than possibilities wrapped in negative attitudes. I commit the work of this day to You and will attempt great things for You because I know I will receive great strength from You.

May I live this day humbly on the knees of my heart, honestly admitting my human inadequacy and gratefully acknowledging Your power. Dwell in the secret places of my heart to give me inner security. Lord, help me to rest in You and receive the incredible resiliency

You provide. Thank You in advance for a truly productive day. In Your all-powerful Name, risen, reigning Christ. Amen.

Limited Expectations

Filled with a strange new hope they came,
The blind, the leper, the sick, the lame.
Frail of body and spent of soul…
As many as touched Him were made whole.

On every tongue was the Healer's name,
Through all the country they spread His fame.
But doubt clung tight to his wooden crutch
Saying, "We must not expect too much."

Down through the ages a promise came,
Healing for sorrow and sin and shame,
Help for the helpless and sight for the blind,
Healing for body and soul and mind.

The Christ we follow is still the same,
With blessings that all who will may claim.
But how often we miss Love's healing touch
By thinking, "We must not expect too much."

AUTHOR UNKNOWN

WHEN I NEED 20/20 HINDSIGHT

I remember the days of old; I meditate on all
Your works; I muse on the work of Your hands.

PSALM 143:5

Gracious Father, help me to live beyond the meager resources of my adequacies and learn that You are totally reliable. When I trust You completely, You constantly lead me into challenges and opportunities that are beyond my strength and experience. I know that in every circumstance You provide me with exactly what I need.

Looking back over my life, I know I could not have made it without Your intervention and inspiration. And when I settle back on a comfortable plateau of satisfaction, suddenly You press me on to new levels of adventure. You are a disturber of false peace, the developer of dynamic character, and the ever-present deliverer when I attempt what I could not do on my own.

Sovereign of my life, I trust You, the ultimate Ruler. Give me acute hindsight so I can have 20/20 vision to see that You are at work in the shadowy realms of the often ambiguous turns of events. I grow in confidence as I remember that You have sustained me in crises at crucial times in my life. There is no panic in heaven; therefore, there can be peace in my soul in the midst of the human muddle of this uncertain time.

You have all power, You alone are almighty, and You are able to accomplish Your purposes and plans. You rule and overrule. When circumstances bring me results that are painful, give me patience to wait for a just resolution. Your intervening power is not limited: You are able to guide me about when and how to do what is best.

May this be a day in which I attempt something beyond my human adequacy and discover that You are able to provide the power to pull it off. Give me a fresh burst of excitement for the duties of this day so that I will be able to serve courageously. I will attempt great things for You and expect great things from You! Amen.

WHEN I NEED TO FORGET SOME
THINGS AND NEVER FORGET OTHERS

God has not given us a spirit of fear but of
power and love and of a sound mind.

2 TIMOTHY 1:7

Dear God, today grant me what You promised: a spirit of power, a spirit of love, and the spirit of a sound mind. I need a sound mind in these tough days. A healed mind. Especially, I need for You to heal my memories and inspire my imagination.

Help me, dear God, to remember to forget some things and never to forget to remember others. I need to allow You to heal the hurting memories of the past: things I've done I should never have done, and things I've said I wish had never been spoken. Equally troubling are the things I wish I had not left unsaid or undone. In this time of honest prayer, I intentionally invite Your Spirit to dredge up memories You want to heal forever. I believe You can do it, Lord! Thank You for the magnificent gift of assurance of pardon.

Now, Lord, energize my imagination. Turpentine the layers of reserve and caution that immobilize my imagination. Clean it all away so I can picture what You want to do in and through me. Help me to see the new person You want me to be. In the same way, show me on the picture screen of my imagination what the people I love would be when filled with Your Spirit, what the situations that trouble me would be with Your solutions, and what the future could be if I let go of my icy grip and put it in Your hands. Thanks for healing me today! Amen.

> I meditate within my heart, and my
> spirit makes diligent search.
>
> PSALM 77:6

> Delight yourself also in the LORD, and He
> shall give you the desires of your heart.
>
> PSALM 37:4

WHEN I NEED TO CHECK
THE BALANCE SHEET

...that the God of our Lord Jesus Christ, the Father
of glory, may give to you the Spirit of wisdom and
revelation in the knowledge of Him, the eyes of your
understanding being enlightened; that you may
know what is the hope of His calling, what are the
riches of the glory of His inheritance in the saints.

EPHESIANS 1:17-18

Gracious Father, source of all my blessings, I am amazed as I check the balance in my spiritual bank account. I begin this new day realizing that You have made an immense deposit of grace, strength, wisdom, and courage in my heart. And what's exciting is that You constantly will replenish my depleted resources throughout the future. Your love has no limits, Your spiritual resilience has no energy crisis, Your hope has no restrictions, and Your power has no ending.

Free me from the false assumption that I am adequate for life's challenges on my own. You promise to go before me. I will encounter no problem for which You have not prepared a solution; I will deal with no person whom You have not prepared to receive a blessing from You through me; I will face no challenge for which You will not make me capable for courageous leadership.

Lord, You know better than I what's ahead. Go before me to show the way. Then meet me in each person and situation. Anoint me with Your Holy Spirit that I may know what to say and do. Help me to anticipate and enjoy Your interventions. Here are my mind, will, and voice. Thank You for Your abiding presence and power. Give me the freedom and joy of knowing that Your special anointing will give me exactly what I need. Thank You for liberating me from the necessity of being adequate on my own. In the name of Christ, I accept Your deposit in my spiritual bank account. There never can be an overdraw! Amen.

Jesus Christ opens wide the doors of the treasure-house of God's promises and bids us go and take what are ours.

CORRIE TEN BOOM

When I Need to Choose to Be Chosen

You are a chosen generation, a royal priesthood, a holy nation, His own special people, that you may proclaim the praises of Him who called you out of darkness into His marvelous light.

1 PETER 2:9

Faithful Father, Your words to Joshua so long ago sound in my soul as Your encouragement to me today. "I will not leave you nor forsake you. Be strong and of good courage." Thank You for the faithfulness and reliability of Your presence. Your love and guidance are not on-again, off-again. I can depend on Your steady flow of strength. Just to know that You are with me in all the ups and downs of life's demands is a great source of confidence. I can dare to be strong in the convictions You have honed in my heart and courageous in the application of them in my relationships and responsibilities.

Infuse my mind with a renewed sense of how much You have invested in me and how much You desire to do through me in the onward movement of Your kingdom.

It is for Your name's sake, Your glory, and Your vision that You bless me. You guide and inspire me because You have great plans for me You want me to accomplish. You have chosen me; may I choose to be chosen today and live with spiritual self-esteem, motivated by this sense of chosenness. Your word for the day is, "Be not afraid, I am with you!" You are my Lord and Savior. Amen. (Joshua 1:5-6.)

> I heard the voice of the LORD, saying, "Whom shall I send, and who will go for Us?" Then I said, "Here am I! Send me."
>
> **ISAIAH 6:8**

> You did not choose Me, but I chose you and appointed you that you should go and bear fruit, and that your fruit should remain, that whatever you ask the Father in My name He may give you.
>
> **JOHN 15:16**

WHEN I NEED TO TRUST MORE

Trust in the LORD with all your heart,
And lean not on your own understanding;
In all your ways acknowledge Him,
And He shall direct your paths.

PROVERBS 3:5-6

Gracious God, You ask from me only what You generously offer to give to me. You initiate this conversation called prayer because You want to bless me with exactly what I will need to live a faithful, confident, productive, joyous life today. You are for me— not against me.

Help me to live the hours of today knowing You are beside, are on my side, and offer me unlimited strength and courage besides. You will provide me insight and inspiration to confront and solve the problems I face. You will give me peace when my heart is distressed by the turbulence of our times. You will comfort me when I am afraid and need Your peace. You make me an overcomer when I feel overwhelmed. In response, I relinquish my imagined control over people and circumstances. I thank You for the power of faith I feel

surging into my mind and heart. I trust in You, dear
God, for You are my Lord and Savior. Amen.

I will love You, O LORD, my strength.
The LORD is my rock and my fortress and my
deliverer; my God, my strength, in whom I will trust.

PSALM 18:1-2

The Spirit Himself bears witness with our spirit
that we are children of God, and if children, then
heirs—heirs of God and joint heirs with Christ, if
indeed we suffer with Him that we may also be
glorified together. For I consider that the sufferings
of this present time are not worthy to be compared
with the glory which shall be revealed in us.

ROMANS 8:16-18

...being confident of this very thing, that He
who has begun a good work in you will
complete it until the day of Jesus Christ.

PHILIPPIANS 1:6

WHEN I NEED A TIME OF ATTITUDE ADJUSTMENT

Your attitude should be the kind that
was shown to us by Jesus Christ.

PHILIPPIANS 2:5 TLB

Gracious God, the source of inner grace and out-ward joy, You have taught me that it is not just my aptitude, but my attitude, that determines the altitude of my success in Your work and in my relationships. I confess that often it is not You but the danger and difficulties of these days that dominate my inner feelings and control my attitudes. It's hard to be up for others when I get down on myself.

So thank You for this attitude adjustment time I call prayer, when I can admit any negative attitudes and submit to the transforming power of Your hope. You have been trying to teach me that true hope is faith in action and the constancy of faith in all contradictory circumstances. You've told me that there is no danger of developing eyestrain from looking at the bright side of things. There is a great need for this quality of hope in our nation. May the attitude of our people toward our present challenges be uplifted by their trust in You, the positive assurance of Your victory over the tyranny of terrorism, and the inspiring attitude of our leaders and all who work with them.

Now in the quiet of this time of honest prayer, I surrender my attitudes to Your transforming power. Give *me* a positive, inspiring attitude. The people around me have a right to see what trust in You can do to a person's attitudes. Make mine a reflection of Your hope and joy. Through Christ the attitude adjuster. Amen.

At the heart of the cyclone tearing the sky,
And flinging the clouds and flowers on,
Is a place of central calm;
And so in the roar of mortal things,
There's a place where my spirit sings,
In the hollow of God's palm.

EDWIN MARKHAM,
FROM *THE SHOES OF HAPPINESS*

WHEN I AM A STINGY RECEIVER

Revive me, O LORD, for Your name's sake! For Your
righteousness' sake bring my soul out of trouble.

PSALM 143:11

Gracious God, sometimes I'm a stingy receiver who
finds it difficult to open my tight-fisted grip on
circumstances and receive the blessings that You have
prepared. You know my needs before I ask You, but
wait to bless me until I ask for Your help. I come to You
now honestly to confess my needs. Lord, I need Your
inspiration for my thinking, Your love for my emotions,
Your guidance for my will, and Your strength for my
body. I've learned that true peace and lasting serenity
result from knowing that You have an abundant supply of resources to help me meet any trying situation,
difficult person, or disturbing complexity, and so I say
with the psalmist, "Blessed be the Lord, who daily loads
us with benefits."

I gladly respond to the admonitions of the psalmist:
"Commit your way to the LORD, trust also in Him, and
He shall bring it to pass…Rest in the LORD, and wait
patiently for Him." I prayerfully accept the vital verbs

of this advice and apply them to my faith today: commit, trust, rest, wait. You have shown me that when I commit to You my life and my challenges, You go into action to bring about Your best for my life. Commitment opens the floodgates of my mind and my heart to the flow of Your power to help with people or problems that concern me.

I trust in Your reliable interventions to free me from anxiety, and when I rest in Your everlasting arms, I experience spiritual resilience and refurbishment. All Your blessings are worth waiting for because nothing else gives me the strength and courage I really need. Thank You for Your faithful reliability. You, dear God, are my Lord and Savior. Amen. (Psalm 68:19; 37:5,7.)

My God shall supply all your need according
to His riches in glory by Christ Jesus.

PHILIPPIANS 4:19

I will keep on being filled with the Spirit.

EPHESIANS 5:18, AUTHOR'S TRANSLATION

WHEN I FEEL LONELY

Lord, it has been an alarming discovery. I can feel lonely in a crowd…when I have lots of friends and when I'm involved in a busy, seemingly productive life. You've helped me discover that loneliness is not the absence of people, but the absence of truly profound relationships in which I can talk out how I'm feeling, share my secrets, and be open about my hopes and dreams. It's also lonely when I don't share with vulnerability my big failures or little goofs.

At the same time, I feel lonely when there's no one with whom I can share my vision for the future, wild and impossible though it may seem at times. I guess a true friend is one with whom I can share the pain that makes me sad and the successes that make me glad. Loneliness seems to get worse when there's not someone who will cry with me and laugh with me, pick me up when life goes "bump," and bring me back down to reality when my plans soar with self-aggrandizement rather than self-sacrifice. I'm talking about true honesty that doesn't just condone, but gently confronts.

Now, Lord, here's the big discovery I'm making: I can't be to others the friend I need them to be to me until I have a truly satisfying relationship with You. Loneliness is the anxiety of unrelatedness. The first step out of it is to trust You as a close confidant. Then help me find people of Your choice to extend the circle, and I'll soon be ready to help heal the multitude of lonely people around me. It's awesome that You want a friend of the likes of me, but You do. You've told me that over and over again. Today, I'm going to believe You! Amen.

I've found a friend; O such a Friend!
He loved me ere I knew Him;
He drew me with the cords of love,
And thus He bound me to Him.
And round my heart still closely twine
Those ties which naught can sever,
For I am His, and He is mine,
Forever and forever.

JAMES GRINDLAY SMALL

WHEN I'M WORRIED

Do not worry about your life, what you will eat or what
you will drink; nor about your body, what you will put
on. Is not life more than food and the body more
than clothing?...For your Heavenly Father knows
that you need all these things. But seek first the
kingdom of God and His righteousness, and all these
things shall be added to you. Therefore do not worry
about tomorrow, for tomorrow will worry about its
own things. Sufficient for the day is its own trouble.

MATTHEW 6:25,32-34

Gracious Father, in whose presence the dark night of
the soul of worry is dispelled by the dawn of Your
love, I thank You for helping me overcome my worries.
You have taught me that worry is like interest paid on
difficulties before it comes due. It's rust on the blade
that dulls my capacity to cut through trouble and lance
the infection of anxiety. Your Word is true: Worry never
changes anything but the worrier, and that change is
never positive. Worry is impotent to change tomorrow
or redo the past. All it does is sap my strength.

I confess that I fear I may have to face alone the
problems and perplexities that come to me. My worry

is really loneliness for You, dear God. In this moment of prayer I surrender all my worries to You and thank You for Your triumphant promise: "Do not be afraid—I will help you. I have called you by name—you are Mine. When you pass through the deep waters, I will be with you; your troubles will not overwhelm you."

In this intimate moment with You, I invite You to help me overcome my worry habit. Grant me fresh strength. I admit my needs and accept Your power. Through Christ who has defeated the destructive power of worry once and for all. Amen. (Isaiah 43:1-2.)

> The LORD your God in your midst, the Mighty One, will save; He will rejoice over you with gladness, He will quiet you with His love, He will rejoice over you with singing.
>
> ZEPHANIAH 3:17

When I Need Meaning in My Work

Whatever you do, do all to the glory of God.

1 CORINTHIANS 10:31

Gracious Father, who has given me life, bless me today in the work I will do. I praise You for work that can be done as an expression of my worship of You. I bring the meaning of my faith to my work rather than trying to make my work the ultimate meaning of my life. With that perspective, I seek to do everything to Your glory.

Fill me with Your grace and make me a cheerful person who makes others happier because I am with them. Make me a blessing and not a burden, a lift and not a load, a delight and not a drag. It's great to be alive! Help me make a difference because of the difference You have made in me.

Sometimes my long days of work and my nights of too little rest run together. I need You. I praise You for Your love that embraces me and gives me security, Your joy that uplifts me and gives me resiliency, Your peace that floods my heart and gives me serenity, and the presence of Your Spirit that fills me and gives me strength and endurance.

I dedicate this day to You. Help me to realize that it is by Your permission that I breathe my next breath, and by Your grace that I am privileged to use all the gifts of intellect and judgment that You provide. Give me a perfect blend of humility and hope, so that I will know You have given me all that I have and am and have chosen to bless me this day. My choice is to respond and to commit myself to You.

I thank You for the attitude change that takes place when I remember I am called to glorify You in my work and to work with excellence to please You. Help me to realize how privileged I am to be able to work, earn wages, and provide for my needs. Thank You for the dignity of work. Whatever I do, in word or deed, I do it to praise You. Amen.

WHEN I FEEL DEPLETED

Humble yourselves under the mighty hand of
God, that He may exalt you in due time, casting
all your care upon Him, for He cares for you.

1 PETER 5:6-7

Almighty God, when I humble myself and confess
my aching need for You, You lift me up and grant
me opportunities beyond my imagination. When I try
to make it on my own, claiming recognition for myself,
eventually I become proud and self-sufficiently arrogant.
Keeping up a front of adequacy becomes demanding.
Pride blocks my relationship with You and debilitates
deep, supportive relationships with others.

I invite You to fill my depleted resources with Your
Spirit. I want to let You love me, forgive me, renew me,
and grant me fresh joy. To this end I admit my needs
and accept Your power.

Thank You, Lord, for the problems that make me
more dependent on You for guidance and strength.
When I have turned to You in the past, You have given
me strength and skills I needed. Thank You for taking
me as I am with all my human weaknesses, and using

me for Your glory. May I always be known for the immensity of my gratitude—my thankfulness for the way that You pour out Your wisdom and vision when I humbly cry out to You for help. I am profoundly grateful. In Christ, my dear Savior's name.

If evil at its overwhelming worst has already been met and mastered, as in Jesus Christ it has; if God has got His hands on this baffling mystery of suffering in its direct, most defiant form, and turned its most awful triumph into uttermost, irrevocable defeat; if that in fact has happened, and on that scale, are you to say it cannot happen on the infinitely lesser scale of our own union with Christ through faith? In heartbreaking things that happen to us, those mental agonies, those spiritual midnights of the soul, we are "more than conquerors," not through our own valor or stoic resolution, not through a creed or code or philosophy, but "through Him who loved us"—through the thrust and pressure of the invading grace of Christ.

JAMES S. STEWART

When I Need to Let Go

Omnipresent Lord God, there is no place I can go where You have not been there waiting for me; there is no relationship in which You have not been seeking to bless the people with whom I am involved; there is no task You have given me to do for which You are not present to help me accomplish. I need not ask to come into Your presence; Your presence with me creates the desire to pray. You delight in guiding me to pray for what You are more ready to give than I may be prepared to ask.

You are here. I do not need to convince You to bless my life. You have shown me how much You love and care. You want the very best for me and have chosen me, through whom You want to work to accomplish Your plans. Help me to see myself as Your agent. Bless me with Your power. Keep me fit physically, secure emotionally, and alert spiritually. So much depends on my trust in You and pursuit of Your guidance. May awe and wonder capture me as I realize all You have put at my disposal to ensure that I succeed. Thank You for the biblical assurance "that all things work together for good to those who love God, to those who are the called according to His purpose." You are my Lord and Savior. Amen. (Romans 8:28.)

May the wisdom of God instruct me,
The eye of God watch over me,
The ear of God hear me,
The word of God give me sweet talk,
The hand of God defend me,
The way of God guide me.
Christ be with me.
Christ before me.
Christ in me.
Christ under me.
Christ over me.
Christ on my right hand.
Christ on my left hand.
Christ on this side.
Christ on that side.
Christ in the head of everyone to whom I speak.
Christ in the mouth of every person who speaks to me.
Christ in the eye of every person who looks upon me.
Christ in the ear of everyone who hears me today.
Amen.

SAINT PATRICK

PART 2

In Times of
Grief and Pain

WHEN I ENDURE GRIEF

God will wipe away every tear from their eyes;
there shall be no more death, nor sorrow,
nor crying. There shall be no more pain, for
the former things have passed away.

REVELATION 21:4

L ord of all life, I come to You for the healing of the
griefs of life. I feel grief whenever I stand in the midst
of shattered dreams. For me, it's essentially my response
to having to say "goodbye" with finality: goodbye at
death's door; goodbye at the collapse of something I've
worked for; goodbye to the past and the what-might-
have-beens of life.

Is there such a thing as "good grief"? Over the years
You have taught me that something is good if it fulfills
its purpose. I'm reluctant to call grief "good" unless it
achieves its intended purpose of healing my disturbed
mind and distressed emotions.

Lord, help me to accept that grief is the healing
process given me as Your gift. I feel pain, and it is
good to know that the process is taking place. When
a loved one dies I experience excruciating reactions. I

tremble, shiver, and feel depleted. I ache emotionally. I'm tempted to have outbursts, or withdraw, deny, or become angry. Most of all I need to find some vent to my anguish. I need to talk to You. Until I know what to say, tears flow. In it all I'm coming to grips with the reality of my loss. And what's truly amazing is that You are there listening and offering Your healing of my grief. Thank You, Lord! Amen.

Nothing can make up for the absence of someone whom we love. It is nonsense to say that God fills the gap; He doesn't fill it, but on the contrary, He keeps it empty and so helps us to keep alive our former communion with each other, even at the cost of pain. The dearer and richer our memories, the more difficult the separation. But gratitude changes the pangs of memory into a tranquil joy. The beauties of the past are borne, not as a thorn in the flesh, but as a precious gift in themselves.

DIETRICH BONHOEFFER

WHEN GRIEF IS NOT AN ENEMY

Blessed are you who weep now, for you shall laugh.

LUKE 6:21

Dear God, You are helping me learn that grief is no more an enemy than is sleep, rest, or the physical healing process of the body. It is Your gift of the cleansing and healing of my emotions. Grief is itself a medicine.

Now I want to thank You for affirming that my grief is an evidence of my capacity to love. Lack of authentic grief is a sign of shallow love and an inability to care deeply. I hear You, Lord! There would be no grief if I did not care. Loss is real, and I feel the pain. It's not a sign of weakness, but of strength.

I need to let my grief flow. With You I can let it out and tell You how I'm really feeling. When I do, I begin to think more clearly about the benefits of eternal life and the dawn of a new day for the one I've lost. This life is but a fraction of eternity; death is not an ending but a transition in living for those who know You through Christ, the cross, and an empty tomb.

And yet, You help me go through the emotional as

well as the thinking process. It is a supreme gift from You to be able to let go and accept my loss. You don't offer shabby shibboleths or trite phrases. You are right here with me: loving, comforting, holding me while I sob. Only after that can I greet the future as a friend. Thank You, eternal healer of grief. Amen.

⁜

There is no circumstance, no trouble, no testing, that can ever touch me until, first of all, it has gone past God and past Christ, right through to me. If it has come that far, it has come with a great purpose, which I may not understand at the moment. But I refuse to become panicky, as I lift up my eyes to him and accept it as coming from the throne of God for some great purpose of blessing to my own heart.

ALAN REDPATH

WHEN GRIEF IS WASTED

No sorrow touches man until it has been
filtered through the heart of God.

JOSEPH BLINCO

Lord, help me not to waste my grief. It is time for growth and for new maturity. Don't let me get caught in the quicksand of "if onlys." If there is something I could or should have done, help me confess that to You and experience Your healing.

Remind me that self-pity is a waste of good grief. "What did I do to deserve this?" or "Why is life treating me so badly?" are irrelevant questions. It's arrogant to barrage You with the silly question, "Why did this happen to me after all the good I've done and the responsible life I've tried to live?" Resentment is equally unproductive. You have been encouraging me to learn that grief can be one of the most creative times in my life.

In the healing of my grief, help me not to make You the enemy. You did not cause my loss, but You are here to help me endure it. Forgive me if I ever blame You and miss Your blessing. I live in a world of germs, illness, and trauma. You don't send trouble; there's already enough to go around. But You have settled the most important issues of life on Calvary, in an Open Tomb, and in an Upper Room at Pentecost. Once again, I accept Your love, and invite Your Spirit to live in me to heal my grief—and I claim that neither death nor anything else can ever separate me from You, now and forever! Amen.

What God Hath Promised

God hath not promised skies always blue, flower-
    strewn pathways all our lives through;
God hath not promised sun without rain, joy
    without sorrow, peace without pain.
God hath not promised we shall not know toil
    and temptation, trouble and woe;
He hath not told us we shall not bear many a
    burden, many a care.

God hath not promised smooth roads and wide,
    swift, easy travel, needing no guide;
Never a mountain rocky and steep, never a river
    turbid and deep.
But God hath promised strength for the day, rest
    for the labor, light for the way,
Grace for the trials, help from above, unfailing
    sympathy, undying love.

ANNIE JOHNSON FLINT

WHEN I NEED TO LET GOD HEAL MY GRIEF

He heals the brokenhearted, binding up their wounds.

PSALM 147:3 TLB

Dear God, the healing power of the world, thank You for helping me realize You don't just send healing of grief. You *are* healing. The healing process of creative grief takes place when I allow You to love me profoundly.

Sometimes this is not easy. When I need You the most I'm tempted to cry out accusingly, "How could You allow this to happen?" When I am honest with You about my feelings, I'm able to think clearly about Your own grief over Your fallen creation and the rebellion of humankind.

I live in a world fractured off from Your original purpose. It is a world filled with suffering. Tragedies occur. Remind me again: You do not send suffering. You grieve because You love me. In Christ You entered into my human grief. Your Son knew the anguish of rejection, hostility, denial, and betrayal, and the suffering of death for the sins of the world.

In times of grief I return to the cross. I cling to the assurance of Your love and forgiveness. Grief alone does not heal me. It is creative only as I receive Your love. Feelings follow thought. I stand on the rock of Christ who lived, died, rose again, and is with me now. Heaven has begun for me. I am alive forever and can face the temporary griefs of life. Amen.

We do not lose heart. Even though our outward man is perishing, yet the inward man is being renewed day by day. For our light affliction, which is but for a moment, is working for us a far more exceeding and eternal weight of glory, while we do not look at the things which are seen, but at the things which are not seen. For the things which are seen are temporary, but the things which are not seen are eternal.

2 CORINTHIANS 4:16-18

WHEN I NEED COURAGE
TO SAY "GOODBYE"

The LORD will be your everlasting light,
and your days of sorrow will end.

ISAIAH 60:20 NIV

Dear Lord, thank You for what You are teaching me about grief. You keep bringing me back to the necessity of eventually saying "goodbye" to a loved one who has graduated to heaven. When I have owned and befriended my grief, have felt through my very human reactions, and have grown in deeper trust in You, there does come a time of release. I think of the Scots expression, "'Bye for just now. See you in the morning!"

Parting is sweet sorrow only when the sweetness is based on the confidence that we will see a loved one again in heaven. For now, however, the physical presence of a loved one is no longer with me. Thank You for cherished memories and for that mystical bond between the living and the graduated in heaven, but free me to live again, making the most of each day until my own graduation.

Thank You for Your ordained duration of mourning.

You do signal me when it is the end of the night. You have all power in heaven and earth to heal me and give me a new beginning when I have the courage to say goodbye to what has been and can never be again. You make me ready to experience what I never dared dream would be possible for the future.

Lord Jesus, You promised, "Blessed are those who mourn, for they shall be comforted." I have mourned and am open to be comforted by You. Your comfort neutralizes the toxins of bitterness and cynicism. Thank You for making me whole! (Matthew 5:4.)

> When this corruptible has put on incorruption, and this mortal has put on immortality, then shall be brought to pass the saying that is written: "Death is swallowed up in victory. O Death, where is your sting? O Hades, where is your victory?"
>
> 1 CORINTHIANS 15:54-55

WHEN I SUFFER WITH CHRIST

My grace is sufficient for you, for My
strength is made perfect in weakness.

2 CORINTHIANS 12:9

Lord Jesus, You told me to abide in You and that You would abide in me. Your indwelling presence turns grim grief into good grief. From within, You assure me I am loved and You give me the power to endure. Thank You for liberating me from within. My relentless questioning—"why, why?"—is replaced by the power to trust that what You have allowed life to give or withhold can be used for my growth in what's ultimately important—my relationship with You. Whatever is my loss, it is more than balanced by the assurance that I'm never called to go through anything that You will not provide strength and courage to conquer.

With awe and wonder I contemplate Paul's bracing truth, "The Spirit Himself bears witness with our spirit that we are children of God, and if children, then heirs—heirs of God and joint heirs with Christ, if indeed [since] we suffer with Him, that we may also be glorified together." Suffering with You, Christ, puts grief into perspective. You are with me and in me. There will be suffering, but You will help me through it. What happens to me can be used for Your glory and for the glory of being made more completely in Your image.

I pause to reflect on all that is mine because I am a joint-heir with You. I belong to the Father's forever family; I am loved and forgiven; I have come alive to life as it was meant to be lived now, and I will live forever; heaven has begun, and fear of death no longer has power over me; I am being transformed into Christ's image; and I have power to confront the problems and perplexities of life. I praise You, Lord! (Romans 8:16-17.)

> As you therefore have received Christ Jesus
> the Lord, so walk in Him, rooted and built
> up in Him and established in the faith.
>
> COLOSSIANS 2:6-7

WHEN I NEED TO COMFORT OTHERS

I will turn their mourning into gladness; I will
give them comfort and joy instead of sorrow.

JEREMIAH 31:13 NIV

Lord, thank You for all You are doing to enable my grief recovery. Now I am ready to be used by You in the lives of others who are suffering from one of the many forms of grief. Put these people on my agenda. Lead me to them. Give me an open, empathetic, and vulnerable spirit willing to share what You have taught me and the healing process through which You have led and continue to lead me.

As I have suffered grief, make me a "wounded healer." I have discovered that my own healing deepens as I care for others. I adopt Paul's prayer as my motto: "Blessed be the God and Father of our Lord Jesus, the Father of mercies and the God of all comfort, who comforts us in all our tribulation, that we may be able to comfort those who are in any trouble, with the comfort with which we ourselves are comforted by God."

Help me remember that I didn't have to take grief alone. You sent me others who shared my grief, told me of how You helped them through their grief, and helped me turn my struggle into a stepping-stone. Lord, I don't want to do any less for the people around me who are suffering. And the wonder of it all is, the more I care for others, the stronger I become.

I've discovered how little people are prepared for the disappointments and discouragements that cause grief. So often they respond as if You are defeated by circumstance, rather than claiming Your power to defeat the enemy of death or the suffering of life. You, dear Christ, have won and are with me to help me claim Your victory. Amen. (2 Corinthians 1:3-4.)

WHEN I ENDURE PHYSICAL PAIN

Christ, I cry out to You in times of physical pain. Bones ache, joints swell, nerves twitch with pulsating waves of pain. You know all about what I endure. It doesn't even compare with the anguish of Your suffering. But what I'm feeling is mine, in my body. I can't take it without the healing touch of Your hand. I yield my pain to You. Please, Lord, take it away, or give me the power to survive the devastating cause of it. I breathe out the pain and breathe in Your Spirit. Thank You for calming my panic.

I think of the time when four men tore a hole in the roof of a house in Capernaum where You were teaching. They lowered down a stretcher with their friend on it. Their deepest desire was to put the man face-to-face with You. I picture the moment his eyes met Yours and You reached out to touch and heal him.

I imagine myself on that stretcher being lowered down before You. Now I look into Your face: wondrous love! I look into Your eyes: compassion, empathy, merciful care. And then I feel the healing hand. It's warm, tender, yet strong and powerful. I feel the surge of Your Spirit enter every facet of my being.

Lord, You are the Healer; You use medicine and doctors and nurses; You work through caregivers. And now I praise You that most of all You give Your healing touch when I need it so much! Amen.

The turning point in our healing often takes place when we surrender our plight to the Lord, relinquish our tenacious grip on our future, and relax in complete trust. Putting our total life under the control of the Master is allowing Him to work out the results according to His plan. After all, we belong to Him whether we live or die. Death is a transition in the midst of eternal life. But in the meantime, the physical problems we face are to be committed to the Lord, placed under His authority, and released for His disposition as He deems best.

WHEN I NEED GOD TO
STAY MY MIND ON HIM

Peace I leave with you, My peace I give to you;
not as the world gives do I give to you. Let not
your heart be troubled, neither let it be afraid.

JOHN 14:37

Gracious God, You promised through Isaiah that "You will keep him in perfect peace, whose mind is stayed on You, because he trusts in You." I need this peace, the peace that passes understanding; the peace that settles my nerves and gives me serenity in these painful times. Your promise through Isaiah reminds me that You are the source of perfect peace, true *sha-lom/shalom*. You stay my mind on You—Your grace and goodness, Your faithfulness, Your resourcefulness, and Your forgiving heart.

Therefore, I commit all my cares and concerns to You. True peace can never be separated from Your Spirit. You are peace! Lasting peace is the result of a heart filled with Your Spirit of peace. Take up residence within me and spread Your peace to every facet of my being. Help me to receive Your gift of peace and hear your message in my soul. *"Shalom/shalom* to you today!" You say.

Dear God, show me what robs me of this wonderful gift. I really want to know, Father, so I can be specific in confession and commitment to change. May Your promises of peace in the Bible become real for me. You know how often I live with anxiety, frustration, and fear. In the quiet of this honest prayer, I open myself for You to teach me the secret of lasting peace. Thank You in advance for whatever it will take to help me receive Your peace so generously offered to me. In the name of the Prince of Peace. Amen. (Isaiah 26:3.)

> It pleased the Father that in Him all the fullness should dwell, and by Him to reconcile all things to Himself, by Him, whether things on earth or in heaven, having made peace through the blood of His cross. And you, who once were alienated and enemies in your mind by wicked works, yet now He has reconciled.
>
> COLOSSIANS 1:19-21

WHEN I NEED TO OVERCOME RATHER THAN BE OVERWHELMED

It's not revolutions and upheavals that
clear the road to new and better days, but
someone's soul inspired and ablaze.

BORIS PASTERNAK

Lord Jesus, what You said to Your disciples on the night before Your crucifixion is the promise I want to claim for this day of my journey through difficult times: "In the world you have tribulation, but *take courage;* I have overcome the world." I hear You whisper in my soul, "Take courage! It's yours!" The imperative is bracing and stirring.

I know I can take hold of the gift of courage, because You have taken a hold of me. "Fear not, I am with you!" are Your courage-inducing words. Fear in these nerve-stretching days drives me to prayer. Courage displaces caution and reserve. I know that nothing can happen that will not bring me closer to You. What You give or withhold always is for my growth. My honest prayers are not an escape from reality and responsibility, but an encounter with them.

Thank You for courage that is based on convictions I cannot deny. You give me courage to act when I know what love demands. You energize my will to put into action costly obedience to You. Courage moves me from panic to Your perspective on things, and then to peace. Give me heightened awareness of what needs to be done, humble attentiveness to Your way to get it done, and honest accountability to You for faithful follow-through. Courage is the greatest virtue You give me because it makes possible all the rest. Today You will give me the power to overcome rather than be overwhelmed. Thank You, Lord! (John 16:33 NASB.)

To every man there openeth
A way, and ways and a way.
And the high soul climbs the high way
And the low soul gropes the low:
And in between, on the misty flats
The rest drift to and fro.
But to every man there openeth
A high way and a low
And every man decideth
The way his soul shall go.

JOHN OXENHAM

PART 3

In Times of Problems

WHEN I WONDER IF GOD
CARES IF I HAVE PROBLEMS

D ear God, years of wrestling with problems have convinced me of a fact of life: I'm like most people in facing one momentous problem—the failure to understand that there is a positive and redemptive purpose to every one of the problems I face. I'm tempted to believe that there is something inherently bad about problems because they often involve me in an inconvenient interruption of my plans for a smooth and successful life.

Problems involve me in unpleasant pressures, distressing conflict, or in physical or emotional pain. I think that freedom from problems should be a reward for hard work, careful planning, and clear thinking. I struggle through the stages of life, battling the problems of getting an education, finding a job, developing a career, raising a family, making ends meet, and eventually retiring. At each stage I look forward to the next period as a time when the problems of life will be behind me. Most disturbing is the assumption that if

I love You, commit my life to You, and diligently try to serve You, You will work things out so I don't have problems.

In this prayer, I want to separate myself from this crowd of people with these perceptions about problems. Your purposes are not thwarted by problems. I'm certain that when You allow a problem, it's because You want me to grow as a person. Actually, often problems define the battle line of Your transforming encounter with ignorance, pride, selfishness, laziness, and resistance to growth. Problems help me reach out to You and allow You to help me find a creative solution and take the next step of becoming a more dynamic person. There's no problem too big for the two of us to solve together! Amen.

Make me a captive, Lord,
And then I shall be free;
Force me to render up my sword,
And I shall conqueror be.
I sink in life's alarms
When by myself I stand;
Imprison me within Thine arms,
And strong shall be my hand.

GEORGE MATHESON

WHEN I FEEL EMPTY

Be steadfast, immovable, always abounding
in the work of the Lord, knowing that
your labor is not in vain in the Lord.

1 CORINTHIANS 15:58

Gracious Lord, I confess the burdens I have tried to carry myself: personal needs, physical tiredness, weariness of living on my own strength, anxiety for the suffering people endure, discouragement in renewing the tradition-bound church, frustration in caring for religious people who may not know You, and anguish over the battle for justice and righteousness in culture. I come empty to be filled, humanly inadequate to be anointed with gifts beyond my talents: a riverbed ready to receive the flow of Your supernatural power. Thank You for loving me as I am, but not leaving me there. Help me press on to live with greater passion than ever before.

You have shown me that the antidote to pride is praise. In this time of prayer, I intentionally praise You for all that I might be tempted to think I have achieved on my own. Pride stunts my spiritual growth and makes me a difficult person for You to bless. Forgive me when

I grasp the glory for myself. Thank You for breaking the bubble of the illusion that I am where I am because of my own cleverness or cunning. Humbly I acknowledge that I could not think a creative thought without Your inspiration and guidance, or accomplish anything of lasting value without Your power and courage. Amen.

> May our Lord Jesus Christ Himself, and our
> God and Father, who has loved us and given
> us everlasting consolation and good hope
> by grace, comfort your hearts and establish
> you in every good word and work.
>
> 2 THESSALONIANS 2:16-17

WHEN I'M BLESSED TO
HAVE PROBLEMS

Take up the whole armor of God, that
you may be able to withstand in the evil
day, and having done all, to stand.

EPHESIANS 6:13

Strong, problem-solving Lord, there is so much in
life I can't be sure of, but Your Word trumpets a
truth I can count on: Irrespective of the intensity of my
problems, You, the Lord of all creation, are with me. In
fact, You've helped me believe that my problems can be
proof of Your recreating presence. You allow problems
to perk to the surface because You are ready to deal
with them through me.

I'm blessed to have problems! You have decided not
to leave me where I am. You've willed to change things,
You're on the move calling me to face relational difficulties, You're helping me understand why some people are
so difficult, You're giving me wisdom to unravel family
problems that have kept me from deeper experiences
of oneness with loved ones. You also call me into cul-
tural battles for truth and righteousness. So, in reality,

a good test of how alive I am is how many soul-sized problems You have allowed me to tackle with Your power and guidance.

The bigger the problem, the more of Your abiding presence I will receive. The more complex the problem, the more advanced will be the wisdom You offer. Equal to the strain of the problem will be the strength that You release. Now I know the hidden truth! It is an evidence of Your presence that You allow problems...to focus the next step of what You want to accomplish in my own life, and accomplish through me in my significant relationships, in my friends, at work, in my church, and in our culture.

I will always have problems. That's life. But I also have You, Lord, who will not only help me grow through them but will give me the power to triumph over them. Amen.

> The weapons of our warfare are not carnal but mighty in God for pulling down strongholds, casting down arguments and every high thing that exalts itself against the knowledge of God, bringing every thought into captivity to the obedience of Christ.
>
> 2 CORINTHIANS 10:4-5

WHEN I AM WEARY

Why are you cast down, O my soul?
And why are you disquieted within me?
Hope in God; For I shall yet praise Him,
The help of my countenance and my God.

PSALM 42:11

Almighty God, reign supreme as sovereign Lord in my life today. Enter my mind and heart and show me the way. May I be given supernatural insight and wisdom to discern Your guidance each step of the way through this challenging day. Break deadlocks with people, enable creative compromises, and inspire a spirit of unity. Overcome the weariness of hard work. Give me a second wind to press on.

When there is nowhere else to turn in my human dilemmas and difficulties, it is time to return to You. When things don't work out, I must ask You to work out things. When my burdens make me downcast, I cast my burdens on You. If You could create the universe and uphold it with Your providential care, You can solve my most complex problems.

Dear Father, I want to know You so well, trust You so completely, seek Your wisdom so urgently, and receive

Your inspiration so intentionally that I will be a person totally available for the influence of Your Spirit. Help me to be just as receptive to Your direction. Alarm me with disquiet in my soul if what I plan is less than Your best. With equal force confirm any conviction that will move forward what You think is best for me. Remind me that You are with me and will guide me. You are Jehovah-Shammah: You will be there! Amen.

I will lift up my eyes to the hills—
From whence comes my help?
My help comes from the LORD,
Who made heaven and earth.
He will not allow your foot to be moved;
He who keeps you will not slumber.
Behold, He who keeps Israel
Shall neither slumber nor sleep.
The LORD is your keeper;
The LORD is your shade at your right hand.
The sun shall not strike you by day,
Nor the moon by night.
The LORD shall preserve you from all evil;
He shall preserve your soul.
The LORD shall preserve your going
out and your coming in
From this time forth, and even forevermore.

PSALM 121

WHEN I NEED
SUPERNATURAL INSIGHT

We...do not cease to pray for you, and to ask that
you may be filled with the knowledge of His will
in all wisdom and spiritual understanding; that
you may walk worthy of the Lord, fully pleasing
Him, being fruitful in every good work and
increasing in the knowledge of God; strengthened
with all might, according to His glorious power,
for all patience and longsuffering with joy.

COLOSSIANS 1:9-11

Gracious Father, Lord of the ups and downs of life, Lord of the seeming triumphs and supposed disappointments, Lord who does not change in the midst of change, I come to You for Your strength and Your power. Make me a hopeful person who expects great strength from You and continues to attempt great strategies for You.

You have called me to be a creative thinker. I begin this day by yielding my thinking brain to Your magnificent creativity. You know everything, You also know what is best for me, and You have entrusted me with responsibilities. I am grateful that You not only are omniscient, but also omnipresent. You are here with me now and will be with me wherever this day's responsibilities take me. I take seriously the admonition of Proverbs, "Commit your works to the LORD, and your thoughts will be established."

Thank You for this secret of success in Your Word. In response I look to what is ahead this day and thank You in advance for supernatural intelligence to maximize my thinking. You are my Lord and Savior. Amen. (Proverbs 16:3.)

> That which was from the beginning, which we have heard, which we have seen with our eyes, which we have looked upon, and our hands have handled, concerning the Word of life—the life was manifested, and we have seen, and bear witness and declare to you that eternal life which was with the Father and was manifested to us—that which we have seen and heard we declare to you, that you also may have fellowship with us; and truly our fellowship is with the Father and with His Son Jesus Christ. And these things we write to you that your joy may be full.
>
> 1 JOHN 1:1-4

WHEN I AM UNDER STRESS

Let the peace of God rule in your hearts.

COLOSSIANS 3:15

Lord, I need Your help. I am feeling the strain of stress. My body is agitated by worry and fear. I confess to You my inability to handle it alone. I surrender my mind to You. Take charge of the control center of my brain. Think Your thoughts through me, and send into my nervous system the pure signals of Your peace, power, and patience. I don't want to have a divided mind fractured off from Your control.

Forgive my angers rooted in petulant self-will. Make me a channel, a riverbed, of Your love to others suffering as much stress as I. Help me act on the inspiration You give me rather than stifling Your guidance.

Take charge of my tongue so it becomes an instrument of healing. Make me a communicator of love and forgiveness as I cheer others on to their best.

I commit my schedule to You, Lord—help me to know and do Your will. Guide me in doing Your will on Your timing so I don't burn out doing the things I don't really want to do, or fear to do what is Your best for me. Set me free from the tyranny of acquisitiveness and the lust of seeking my security in things rather than in my relationship with You.

I long to be the person You created me to be, and not anyone else. Forgive me when I take my signals of success from others and not You.

Most of all, Lord, help me to catch the drumbeat of Your guidance and live by Your timing. Here is my life—invade it, fill it, transform it. And I thank You in advance for the healing of my life and for giving me strength to conquer stress. Amen.

WHEN I NEED WISDOM

If any of you lacks wisdom, let him ask of
God, who gives to all liberally and without
reproach and it will be given to him.

JAMES 1:5

Immortal, invisible, God only wise, in light inaccessible hid from my eyes, I confess my lack of wisdom to solve the problems I'm facing. The best of my education, experience, and erudition is not enough. I turn to You and ask for the gift of wisdom. You never tire of offering it, I desire it, and these times require it.

I am stunned by the qualifications of receiving wisdom. Proverbs reminds me that the secret is creative fear of You. What does it mean to fear You? You have taught me that it is really awe, wonder, and humble adoration. My profound concern is that I might be satisfied with my surface analysis and be unresponsive to Your offer of wisdom. Lord, grant me the knowledge and understanding of Your wisdom so that I may speak Your words on my lips. When nothing less will do, You give wisdom to those who humbly ask for it. Thank You, God. Amen.

I thank You and praise You, O God of my fathers;
You have given me wisdom and might.

DANIEL 2:23

Do not be wise in your own opinion.

ROMANS 12:16

The wisdom of God that is from above is
first pure, then peaceable, gentle, willing to
yield, full of mercy and good fruits, without
partiality and without hypocrisy.

JAMES 3:17

Knowledge is horizontal. Wisdom is
vertical—it comes down from above.

BILLY GRAHAM

WHEN I AM TROUBLED

Hear my prayer, O LORD. Do not hide Your face from
me in the day of my trouble; incline Your ear to me.

PSALM 102:1

Gracious God, a very present help in trouble, I praise
You for giving me Your tenacity to live through
troubled times. I listen in on Your conversation with the
psalmist when he was beset with trouble. I hear Your
gracious invitation: "Call on Me in the day of trouble;
I will deliver you, and you shall glorify Me." I respond
in faith with the psalmist, "Though I walk in the midst
of trouble, You will revive me."

Thank You, Lord, for Your reviving power. You
revive me with convictions that cannot be compro-
mised: You are my refuge and our strength; You have
blessed our nation through our history; You will help
us be victorious over the evil of those who wish us harm.
I am revived also by the replenishing of my confidence:
You will save me through my present crisis; I need not
fear. I feel Your Spirit surging into my soul: anxiety is
replaced by serene security, frustration by faith, tiredness with tenacity, and caution with courage. And so

I say with the psalmist, "In the day when I cried out, You answered me, and made me bold with strength in my soul." Amen. (Psalm 50:15; 138:7; 138:3.)

Passing Through

"When Thou passest through the waters," deep the
    waves may be, and cold,
But Jehovah is our refuge and His promise is our
    hold;
For the Lord Himself hath said it, He the faithful
    God and true;
When thou comest to the waters, Thou shalt *not go
down*, but *through*.

Threatening breakers of destruction, doubt's insidi-
    ous undertow,
Shall not sink us, shall not drag us out to ocean
    depths of woe;
For His promise shall sustain us, praise the Lord,
    whose word is true!
We shall not go down or under, He hath said, "Thou
    passest *through*."

ANNIE JOHNSON FLINT

WHEN I NEED CONFIDENCE
IN GOD'S CONTROL

Though I walk in the midst of
trouble, You will revive me.

PSALM 138:7

Almighty God, in these uncertain days, I want to reaffirm some very powerful presuppositions about You and Your providential care for Your creation. Strengthen my conviction that You do not cause tragedies. I dismiss that false question, "Where was God in the midst of the disaster?" You were with us giving us courage and hope.

You created humankind—to know, to love, and to serve You. I reverently reflect on what must have been Your most crucial decision when You created humankind: You gave us freedom of choice, knowing that there can be no response of love without choice, but also that humankind would abuse this freedom. There is an objective force of evil in the world that often has been expressed through people, and movements, and nations. Heinous acts happen.

You are not dissuaded. You suffer with me and,

in ways I could not plan, bring good out of evil. Not even death can separate me from You. This life is but a small part of the whole of eternity. In the midst of my anguish over those who die in tragedies, remind me of the shortness of time and the length of eternity. Make me a communicator of love and strength to those who continue to suffer in the grim outbursts of evil deeds. Bless all of us with a fresh gift of faith to trust You, and a renewed assurance that "though the wrong seems oft so strong, You are the ruler yet!" Amen.

You are great, and do wondrous things;
You alone are God.

PSALM 86:10

Blessed be the God and Father of our Lord
Jesus Christ, the Father of mercies and God
of all comfort, who comforts us in all our
tribulation, that we may be able to comfort those
who are in any trouble, with the comfort with
which we ourselves are comforted by God.

2 CORINTHIANS 1:3-4

WHEN BAD THINGS HAPPEN

Why do you boast in evil, O mighty man? The
goodness of God endures continually.

PSALM 52:1

Lord, when things go bad, I urgently need a fresh experience of Your goodness. You are always consistent, never changing, constantly fulfilling Your plans and purposes, and totally reliable. There is no shadow of turning with You; as You have been, You will be forever. All Your attributes are summed up in Your goodness. It is the password for Your presence, the metonym for Your majesty, and the synonym for Your strength. Your goodness is the generosity that You define. It is Your outrushing, unqualified love poured out in graciousness and compassion. You are good when circumstances seem bad. When I ask for Your help, Your goodness can bring what is best out of the most complicated problems.

Dear God, Your mercies are indefatigable, and Your presence sustains me through the day. I seek to glorify You in all I do and say. You provide me strength for this day, guidance in my decisions, vision for the way, courage in adversity, help from above, unfailing empathy, and unlimited love. You never leave me nor forsake me, nor do You ask of me more than You will provide the resources to accomplish.

Thank You for Your goodness given so lavishly to me in the past. Today, again I turn to You for Your guidance for what is good for me, my family, and my friends. Keep me grounded in Your sovereignty, rooted in Your commandments, and nurtured by the absolutes of Your truth and righteousness. May Your goodness always be the source of the graciousness I long to be able to express today. In the good name of Jesus, my Lord and Savior. Amen.

I would have lost heart, unless I had
believed that I would see the goodness
of the LORD in the land of the living.

PSALM 27:13

We know that all that happens to us is working for our
good if we love God and are fitting into His plans.

ROMANS 8:28 TLB

WHEN I AM TIRED

I will love You, O LORD, my strength.
The LORD is my rock and my fortress and my deliverer;
My God, my strength, in whom I will trust;
My shield and the horn of my salvation, my stronghold.

PSALM 18:1-2

Gracious Father, in troublesome days of conflict and consternation, frustration and fatigue, stress and strain, I come to You seeking Your special tonic for tiredness. I am feeling the energy-sapping tension of this time. I claim Your promise, "As your days, so shall your strength be." Your strength is perfectly matched for whatever life will dish out today. You promise me the stamina of ever-increasing fortitude. In the quiet of this communion with You, I open the floodgates of my soul and ask You to flood my mind with a refreshing renewal of hope in You, my emotions with a calm confidence in help from You, and my body with invigorating health through You.

I thank You, mighty God, Creator of the universe and Re-creator of those who trust You, for this most crucial appointment of the day with You. You have commanded that I be still and know that You are God. Lift my burdens, show me solutions to my problems, and give me the courage to press on. Through Christ my overcoming Lord. Amen. (Deuteronomy 33:25.)

I will call upon the LORD, who is worthy to be praised.

PSALM 18:3

The hour is coming, and now is, when the true worshipers will worship the Father in spirit and truth; for the Father is seeking such to worship Him. God is Spirit, and those who worship Him must worship in spirit and truth.

JOHN 4:23-24

You are worthy, O Lord, To receive glory and honor and power; For You created all things, And by Your will they exist and were created.

REVELATION 4:11

He has shown you, O man, what is good; And what does the LORD require of you But to do justly, to love mercy, And to walk humbly with your God?

MICAH 6:8

WHEN I NEED TO BE OPTIMISTIC

The future is as bright as the promises of God.

ADONIRAM JUDSON

Gracious God, give me an assurance of Your unqualified love, profound peace that quiets my heart, and ears tuned to hear Your song of affirmation. I need Your gift of vibrant optimism.

My optimism often is like a tea bag; I never know how strong it is until I get into hot water. In times of frustration or adversity my optimism is tested. When the wheels of organization grind slowly, often I become pessimistic. It is then I need to hear Your song of encouragement. So often I live as if I had to carry the burdens of leadership alone. Today I relinquish to You any negative thoughts, critical attitudes, and impatient moods. Infuse me with Your hope. Again I pray, hope through me today, O God of hope, so that my discouragements will be turned to optimism based on Your faithfulness. "Ring out the bells of the kirk; God is down to Earth to bless those who work!"

Thank You, dear God, that You are closer than my hands and feet and as available for inspiration as my breathing. May this day be lived in companionship with You, so that I will enjoy the confidence of the promise You gave through Isaiah: "It shall come to pass that before they call, I will answer; and while they are still speaking, I will hear."

When this day closes, my deepest joy will be that I have worked to achieve Your goals. You are my Lord and Savior, the Source of true optimism. Amen. (Isaiah 65:24.)

> You are my rock and my fortress:
> Therefore, for Your name's sake,
> Lead me and guide me.
>
> PSALM 31:3

May the road rise up to meet you
May the wind be always at your back,
May the sun lie warm upon your face,
The rain fall softly on your fields
And until we meet again
May the Lord hold you
In the hollow of His hand.

GAELIC BLESSING

When I Need a Fresh Touch

*When you pray, go into your room, and when you
have shut your door, pray to your Father who is in
the secret place; and your Father who sees in secret
will reward you openly. And when you pray, do not
use vain repetitions as the heathen do. For they
think that they will be heard for their many words.
Therefore do not be like them. For your Father knows
the things you have need of before you ask Him.*

MATTHEW 6:6-8

Almighty God, in challenging days I remember Abraham Lincoln's words, "I have been driven many times upon my knees by the overwhelming conviction that I had nowhere else to go. My own wisdom, and that of all about me, seemed insufficient for the day."

Holy, righteous God, I sense that same longing to be in profound communion with You because I need vision, wisdom, and courage no one else can provide. I long, with Lincoln, for my prayers to be a consistent commitment to be on Your side rather than an appeal for You to join my causes. Forgive me when I act like I have a corner on the truth and always am right. Then my prayers reach no further than the ceiling. In humility,

I spread out my concerns before You and ask for Your inspiration. You have taught me to pray, "Your will be done on earth as it is in heaven."

Dear God, I do not need to ask to come into Your presence, for You have been ever-present through my nights and days. I never need shout across the spaces to You as an absent God. You are nearer than my own soul and closer than my most secret thoughts. I need not inform You of my requests, for You are omniscient. I do not need to brief You on the alternative possibilities for today's decisions, for You already know what is in keeping with Your best for me and will reveal that if I ask You.

What I do need is to linger in Your presence until I am assured of Your love, regain true security, and am refortified by Your strength. Thank You for using this time of prayer with You to show me Your faithfulness and to give me Your guidance. Amen.

PART 4

In Times of
Trying Relationships

WHEN I NEED TO
COMMUNICATE LOVE

Love is patient, love is kind...it does not seek its own.

1 CORINTHIANS 13:4-7 NASB

O God of love, give me a fresh experience of Your love today. Help me to think about how much You love me with unqualified acceptance and forgiveness. May the tone and tenor of my words to the people in my life be an expression of Your love. You have called me to love as You have loved me. Help me to love those with whom I find it difficult to bear and those who find it a challenge to bear with me.

Show me practical ways to express love in creative ways. May I lift burdens rather than become one; may I add to people's strength rather than being a source of stress. Place on my agenda the particular people to whom You have called me to communicate Your love. And give me that resolve of which great days are made: *If no one else does, Lord, I will!*

Place in my mind loving thoughts and feelings for the people in my life. Show me caring things I can do to enact what's in my heart. Direct specific acts of caring You have motivated in my heart. Don't let me forget, Lord. Give me the will to act, to say what I feel. Through Him who is Your amazing Grace. Amen.

A Caring Covenant

1. I will begin each day with an unreserved commitment of my life to Christ,

2. I will invite Christ to fill me with His Spirit: my mind to think His thoughts, my emotions to express His love, and my will to discern and do His will.

3. I will focus on the specific opportunities and challenges in my relationships and responsibilities in the day ahead, and will surrender each of these to Christ and ask for supernatural power, wisdom, and guidance.

4. I promise to pray for people on my heart by name, picturing them and asking for Christ's special empowering. During the day, as they are brought to my mind or I learn of special needs, I will accept these as nudges to intercede for them.

5. I will end the day with a time of reflection on how the Lord blessed and empowered me and others so that gratitude and praise will conclude each day.

WHEN PEOPLE I LOVE ARE
IN TROUBLE BECAUSE OF
SEPARATION FROM GOD

Dear God, today I want to pray for the people You have put on my prayer agenda who are in trouble because of sin in their lives. I know the pain and anguish my own sins have caused me and other people. Out of gratitude and praise for Your forgiveness of me, I want to pray for people I love. Lord, before it's too late, open their hearts to Your love. Show me how I can be part of Your pursuit of them. Enable me to know what to do and say, when and how I am to incarnate Your love by intervening with comfort or confrontation.

Dear God, thank You for not tolerating the sin of the world. Because You cared, You came in Jesus Christ to reconcile us to Yourself. You did not tolerate my rebellion, but invaded me with love and forgiveness. Give me the courage to do more than tolerate people. Help me to remember what life was like before I knew You personally. May that shock me out of bland aloofness from the peril in which people around me are living. Thank You for giving me joy and hope to share. Clarify for me the people in my life who have been prepared by You for a loving and decisive confrontation.

Gracious God, You also have shown me what authentic graciousness is. I want to live this day as a gracious person. You have made me a host for the strangers of the world. I commit the hours of this day to hospitality. Flow through my words and actions as I meet people who are strangers because of their estrangement from You. I offer an open heart to welcome them in Your name. Amen.

More things are wrought by prayer
Than this world dreams of.
Wherefore, let thy voice
Rise like a fountain for me night and day.
For what are men better than sheep or goats
That nourish a blind life within the brain,
If, knowing God, they lift not hands of prayer
Both for themselves and those who call them
        friend?
For so the whole round earth is every way
Bound by gold chains about the feet of God.

ALFRED, LORD TENNYSON,
FROM *IDYLLS OF THE KING*

WHEN JUDGMENTS DIVIDE

Let us not judge one another anymore.

ROMANS 14:13

Almighty God, You have created me in Your own image; forgive me when I return the compliment by trying to create You in my image, projecting onto You my human judgmentalism. I evade Your judgment of my judgments. My judgments divide me from others. I condemn those who differ with me; I miss Your lordship by lording it over others.

I need to be reconciled to You, Lord. Forgive any pride, prejudice, and presumption. People are deeply wounded by cutting words and hurting attitudes toward their religions, races, and political parties. Life is divided into camps of liberal and conservative, this party or that party, and from each camp we shout demeaning criticism of each other.

Forgive my arrogance, but also forgive my reluctance to work together with those with whom I differ. I confess that Your work is held back because of intolerance. I also know that You are the instigator of my longing to be one with You and the inspiration of oneness. Bind me together with others with the triple-braided cord of Your acceptance, atonement, and affirmation.

God of peace, I seek to receive Your peace and communicate it to others throughout this day. I confess anything that may be disturbing my inner peace. I know that if I want peace in my heart, I cannot harbor resentment. I seek forgiveness for any negative criticism, gossip, or innuendo I may have spoken. Forgive the times I have brought acrimony into my relationships instead of bringing peace into misunderstandings. You have shown me that being a reconciler is essential for a continued, sustained experience of Your peace. Most of all, I know that lasting peace results from Your indwelling Spirit, Your presence in my mind and heart.

Show me how to become a communicator of the peace that passes understanding, bringing healing reconciliation, deeper understanding, and open communication. In the name of the Prince of peace, Jesus Christ our Lord. Amen.

A man's judgment of another depends more on the one judging and on his passions than on the one being judged and on his conduct.

PAUL TOURNIER

When I Need Reconciliation

Almighty God, I confess anything that stands between me and You and between me and anyone else. I long to be in a right relationship with You again. I know the love, joy, and peace that flood my being when I am reconciled with You. I become a riverbed for the flow of Your supernatural gifts of leadership: wisdom, knowledge, discernment, vision, and authentic charisma.

I confess the pride that estranges me from You and the judgmentalism that strains my relationships. Forgive my cutting words and hurting attitudes toward other religions or races and people with different beliefs, political preferences, or convictions on issues. So often people are divided into camps and opposing groups and I am critical of those with whom I disagree. Help me to express to others the grace I have received in being reconciled to You.

May my efforts to reach out to others be a way of telling You how much I love You. In the Name of Christ who gave me the eleventh commandment, His own: "A new commandment I give to you, that you love one another; as I have loved you, that you also love one another." Amen. (John 13:34.)

> If anyone is in Christ, he is a new creation; old things have passed away; behold, all things have become new. Now all things are of God, who has reconciled us to Himself through Jesus Christ, and has given us the ministry of reconciliation, that is, that God was in Christ reconciling the world to Himself, not imputing their trespasses to them, and has committed to us the word of reconciliation. Now then, we are ambassadors for Christ, as though God were pleading through us: we implore you on Christ's behalf, be reconciled to God. For He made Him who knew no sin to be sin for us, that we might become the righteousness of God in Him.
>
> 2 CORINTHIANS 5:17-21

WHEN I NEED TO BE SENSITIVE TO THE NEEDS OF OTHERS

A new commandment I give to you, that you love
one another; as I have loved you, that you also
love one another. By this all will know that you are
My disciples, if you have love for one another.

JOHN 13:34-35

Loving God, You have blessed me so that I may be
a vital part of Your blessing to others. I commit
myself to be sensitive to the needs of others around me.
Show me the people who particularly need encouragement or affirmation. Give me exactly what I should say
to uplift them. Free me of preoccupation with myself
and my own needs. Help me to remember that people
will care about *what* I know when they know I care
about them. May my countenance, words, and actions
communicate my caring. Make me a good listener and
enable me to hear what people are expressing beneath
what they are saying.

Most of all, remind me of the power of intercessory
prayer. May I claim Your best for people as I pray for
them. Especially I pray for those with whom I disagree

on issues. Help me to see them not as enemies but as people who will help sharpen my edge. Lift me above petty attitudes or petulant gossip. Fill this day with Your presence, and my heart with Your magnanimous attitude toward others.

Enlarge my heart until it is big enough to contain the gift of Your Spirit; expand my mind until I am capable of thinking Your thoughts; deepen my trust so I can live with freedom from anxiety. I commit my life into Your capable hands. Amen.

> Jesus said to Simon Peter, "Simon, son of Jonah, do you love Me more than these?" He said to Him, "Yes, Lord; You know that I love You." He said to him, "Feed My lambs."
>
> JOHN 21:15

WHEN I NEED TO MAKE
A FRESH START

Gracious Father, giver of every good gift for my growth as Your child, I acknowledge my utter dependence on You. I have nothing I have not received from You. You sustain me day by day, moment by moment. I deliberately empty my mind and heart of anything that does not glorify You. I release to You any pride, self-serving attitude, or willfulness I may have harbored in my heart. I ask You to take from me anything that makes it difficult not only to love, but to like, certain people. May my relationships reflect Your initiative, love, and forgiveness.

Dear God, so often in my prayers I present You with my own agenda. I ask for guidance and strength and courage to do what I have already decided. Usually, what I have in mind is to receive from You what I think I need in order to get on with my prearranged plans. Often I present my shopping list of the blessings I have in mind for my projects, many of which I may not have checked out with You in the first place. Sometimes I make little time to talk to You or listen to You.

I want to be all that You want me to be, and I want to do what You have planned for me. May this prayer be the beginning of a conversation with You that lasts all through the day. Help me to attempt something I could not do without Your power. In the name of Christ who calls me to admit my need, submit my failures, and commit my life to make a fresh start. Amen.

Recapitulation, Resurrection, Regeneration:
Three momentous words; words of great hope.
Christ's death and resurrection are recapitulated in
    us when we surrender our lives to Him.
We die to self-sovereignty; we are born again.
A new person is raised up in us,
We are a new creature.
A new creation.
Old things pass away, the new has come. We are
    ready to be filled with the Holy Spirit.
Our regeneration begins. Each day we are filled
    afresh. Our transformation continues.
We have been called, chosen, destined to be made
    like Christ.
Fear of death is gone; all our physical death can
    do to us is to release us to a fuller realization
    of heaven we have begun to experience now.

WHEN MY MOTIVES
NEED MENDING

O LORD, You have searched me and known me.
You know my sitting down and my rising up;
You understand my thought afar off.
You comprehend my path and my lying down,
And are acquainted with all my ways.

PSALM 139:1-3

Almighty God, ultimate judge of my life, in this
moment of quiet reflection, I hold up my motives
for Your review. I want to be totally honest with You and
with myself about what really motivates my decisions,
words, and actions. Sometimes I want You to approve
of motives I have not even reviewed in light of Your
righteousness, justice, and love. There are times when
I am driven by self-serving motives that contradict my
better nature.

Most serious of all, I confess that sometimes my
motives are dominated by secondary loyalties: ambi-
tion blurs my vision; combative competition prompts
manipulative methods; negative attitudes foster strained
relationships. I ask You to purify my motives and refine

them until they are in congruity with Your will and Your vision for my life. When I put You first in my life, You bring results I could not achieve by human methods alone. I thank You in advance for performing these miracles.

Sovereign God, You are my help in all the ups and downs of life, all the triumphs and defeats, and all the changes and challenges. You are my Lord in all seasons and for all reasons. I can come to You when life makes me glad or sad. There is no circumstance beyond Your control. Wherever I go, You are there waiting for me. You are already at work with people before I encounter them. You prepare solutions for my complexities, and You are always ready to help me resolve conflicts even before I ask.

My only goal is to please You in what I say and accomplish. Give me Your strength to endure and Your courage to triumph in things great and small that I attempt for the good of all. In Christ's name. Amen.

Search me, O God, and know my heart;
Try me, and know my anxieties;
And see if there is any wicked way in me,
And lead me in the way everlasting.

PSALM 139:23-24

WHEN I LONG FOR RENEWED PURPOSE

It is awesome and breathtaking. God has created
us a little lower than Himself and is mindful of us
so we can be mindful of Him and responsive
to His calling for us to have dominion over the
work of His hands. He has crowned us with glory
and honor. In response, we claim our realm of
responsibility, commit ourselves to servant leadership
in our realm, and count on supernatural power
to accomplish His purpose for us in our realm.

The psalmist draws my heart and mind to You, dear
God:

"O LORD, our Lord, how excellent is Your name in
all the earth...What is man that You are mindful of him,
and the son of man that You visit him? For You have
made him a little lower than the angels, and You have
crowned him with glory and honor. You have made him
to have dominion over the works of your hands."

Gracious God, ultimate Sovereign and Lord of my
life, I am stunned again by Your majesty and the mag-
nitude of the delegated dominion You have entrusted to
me. I respond with awe and wonder and with renewed

commitment to be a servant leader. In a culture that often denies Your sovereignty and worships at the throne of the perpendicular pronoun—"I"—help me to exemplify the greatness of servanthood. You have given me a life full of opportunities to serve, freed me more and more from self-serving aggrandizement, and enabled me to live at full potential for Your glory. I humble myself before You and acknowledge that I could not breathe a breath, think a thought, make a decision, or press on to excellence without Your power. By Your appointment I am where I am doing the work You have given me to do: called to serve others. Grant me grace and courage to give myself away to You and to others with whom I am privileged to live and work today. Amen. (Psalm 8:1,4-6.).

To me, to live is Christ.

PHILIPPIANS 1:21

I press on, that I may lay hold of that for which Christ Jesus has also laid hold of me.

PHILIPPIANS 3:12

I have fought the good fight, I have finished the race, I have kept the faith.

2 TIMOTHY 4:7

WHEN PRAISE IS THE ANSWER

Sing to the LORD, all the earth;
Proclaim the good news of His
salvation from day to day.
Declare His glory among the nations,
His wonders among all peoples.
For the LORD is great and greatly to be praised.

1 CHRONICLES 16:23-25

Blessed God, my Father, You have shown me that there is great spiritual power in praise. When I praise You, my mind and heart are opened to Your Spirit, burdens are lifted, problems are resolved, and strength is released. So I join my voice with the psalmist: "I will tell of all Your marvelous works. I will be glad and rejoice in You; I will sing praise to Your name, O Most High."

I confess that often it is difficult to praise You in troublesome times and with frustrating people. And yet, it is when I deliberately praise You for them that I receive fresh inspiration. Help me remember what You have taught me: Praising You for the most challenging situations and contentious people transforms me and my attitudes, as well as them.

Give me greater confidence in Your inner working in people and in Your unseen but powerful presence in every situation. Again I join the psalmist, "Because Your lovingkindness is better than life, my lips shall praise You. Thus I will bless You while I live." This is a day to praise You, O Lord! Amen. (Psalm 9:1-2; 63:3-4.)

Oh, give thanks to the Lord!
Call upon His name;
Make known His deeds among the peoples!
Sing to Him, sing psalms to Him;
Talk of all His wondrous works!
Glory in His holy name;
Let the hearts of those rejoice who seek the Lord!
Seek the Lord and His strength;
Seek His face evermore!

1 CHRONICLES 16:8-11

PART 5

IN TIMES WHEN GOD
HIMSELF IS THE ANSWER

WHEN I NEED GOD HIMSELF
MORE THAN HIS GIFTS

God of Your Goodness, give me Yourself, for You
are sufficient for me...If I were to ask anything less I
should always be in want, for in You alone do I have all.

JULIAN OF NORWICH

Loving Father, I come to You seeking the ultimate joy of life: I simply come to abide simply in Your presence. I would not interrupt what You have to say to me with chatter. I need You more than anything that You can provide for me. Make me as ready to listen as I am to talk. You have created me for communion with You. I thank You for speaking to me in my soul. Now I hear what You have been seeking to tell me: I am loved, forgiven, and cherished by You. You have plans for me and a personal will for me. I open my mind and heart to receive You—my Lord, Savior, Peace, and Power.

Your presence is with me even when I become busy and momentarily forget You. Thank You for continually breaking through the barriers of insensitivity with the overtures of Your love. You are my closest Friend, as well as my God. Help me to keep that friendship in good working order. Lord, You know me. I get so absorbed in my activities and begin to think I am capable of functioning without Your strength. Show me the mediocrity of my efforts without Your interventions and inspiration. I dedicate this day to live for Your glory and by Your grace, sustained by Your goodness. You are my Lord and Savior. Amen.

> Abide in Me, and I in you. As the branch cannot
> bear fruit of itself, unless it abides in the vine,
> neither can you, unless you abide in Me.
>
> **JOHN 15:4**

> By this we know that we abide in Him, and He
> in us, because He has given us of His Spirit.
>
> **1 JOHN 4:13**

> As the deer pants for the water brooks, so
> pants my soul for You, O God. My soul
> thirsts for God, for the living God.
>
> **PSALM 42:1-2**

> Because Your lovingkindness is better than life, my
> lips shall praise You. Thus I will bless You while I live.
>
> **PSALM 63:3-4**

When My Inner Eyes Need Focus

Silently now I wait for Thee
Ready, my God, Thy will to see
Open my eyes, illumine me,
Spirit divine.

CLARA H. SCOTT

Almighty God, it is with Your permission that I am alive, by Your grace that I have been prepared for my work, by Your appointment that I am here, and by Your blessing that I am secure in the gifts and talents that You have given me. Renew my body with health and strength. Open my inner eyes so I can see things and people with Your perspective. Teach me new truth today. May I never be content with what I have learned or think I know. Set me free to soar with wings of joy and delight. I trade in the spirit of self-importance for the spirit of self-sacrifice, the need to appear great for the desire to make others great, the worry over my place of importance for the certainty of Your place in my heart. Restore the continuous flow of Your Spirit through me as a mighty river.

Dear God, You promise to be with me whenever

and wherever I need You throughout this day. You have assured me that You will never leave or forsake me. You remind me that Your love is there when I am insecure, Your strength when I am stretched beyond my resources, Your guidance when I must make decisions. Your hope when I am tempted to be discouraged, Your patience when difficult people distress me, Your joy when I get grim.

I open my mind to receive Your divine intelligence, my responsibilities to glorify You, my relationships to express Your amazing affirmation, my face to radiate Your care and concern. As You care for me today, I pledge myself to live for Your glory. I am ready to receive what I will need each hour—each challenge, each opportunity. This day is a gift, and I accept it gratefully. You are my Lord and Savior. Amen.

Be Thou my Vision, O Lord of my heart;
Naught be all else to me, save that Thou art
Thou my best Thought, by day or by night,
Waking or sleeping, Thy presence my light.

IRISH, TRANSLATED BY MARY BYRNE

WHEN I NEED TO SEE THE INVISIBLE IN THE VISIBLE

How precious also are Your thoughts to me,
O God! How great is the sum of them!

PSALM 139:17

Almighty God, help me to see the invisible movement of Your Spirit in people and events. Beyond my everyday world of ongoing responsibilities and the march of secular history with its sinister and frightening possibilities, You call me to another world of suprasensible reality, which is the mainspring of the universe, the environment of everyday existence, and my very life and strength at this moment. Help me to know that You are present, are working Your purposes out, and have plans for me. Give me eyes to see Your invisible presence working through people, arranging details, solving complexities, and bringing good out of whatever difficulties I entrust to You.

I begin this new day affirming my loyalty to You, dear God. Grant me eyes to see You as the unseen but ever-present Sovereign. Then help me to claim Your promise, "Call to Me, and I will answer you, and show

you great and mighty things, which you do not know."
Through Christ my Lord and Savior. Amen. (Jeremiah
33:3.)

To them God willed to make known what are the
riches of the glory of this mystery among the
Gentiles: which is Christ in you, the hope of glory.

COLOSSIANS 1:27

Now to the King eternal, immortal,
invisible, to God who alone is wise, be
honor and glory forever and ever.
Amen.

1 TIMOTHY 1:17

I will bring the blind by a way they did not know;
I will lead them in paths they have not known.
I will make darkness light before them,
And crooked places straight.
These things I will do for them,
And not forsake them.

ISAIAH 42:16

The LORD is near to all who call upon Him, to
all who call upon Him in truth. He will fulfill
the desire of those who fear Him.

PSALM 145:18-19

When I Need to Wait on God

D ear God, think Your thoughts through me today. I want to love You with my mind and praise You with my intellect. I seek to be a riverbed for the mighty flow of Your wisdom through me. Teach me to wait on You, to experience deep calm of soul, and then to receive Your guidance. I spread out before You the decisions I must make. Thank You in advance for Your guidance. Give me the humility to trust You for answers and solutions, and then grant me the courage to do what time alone with You has convinced me must be done. You are the author of all truth and the bottomless sea of understanding.

Send Your Spirit into my mind and illuminate my understanding with insight and discernment. I accept the admonition of Proverbs, "Incline your ear to wisdom, and apply your heart to understanding; yes, if you cry out for discernment, and lift up your voice for understanding, if you seek her as silver, and search for her as for hidden treasures; then you will understand the fear of the LORD, and find the knowledge of God. For the LORD gives wisdom; from His mouth come knowledge and understanding." Amen. (Proverbs 2:2-6.)

There are days of silent sorrow
In the seasons of our life;
There are wild despairing moments.
There are hours of mental strife;
There are times of stony anguish,
When the tears refuse to fall;
But the waiting time, my brothers,
Is the hardest time of all…
We can bear the heat of conflict,
Though the sudden, crushing blow,
Beating back our gathered forces,
For a moment lay us low;
We may rise again beneath it
None the weaker for the fall,
But the waiting time, my brothers,
Is the hardest time of all.

SARA DOUDNEY

WHEN I NEED A
HEALING OF MEMORIES

Do you want to be made well?

JOHN 5:6

Christ, the healer of memories, thank You for clearing the memories I harbor of my failures, mistakes, and inadequacies. I know if those memories are not forgiven and cleansed, they will fester in me. Eventually they will congeal into an overall attitude of self-condemnation or dread. I need to hear and appropriate your words: "Neither do I condemn you." Then I need to say that to myself—and finally, to people who may have hurt me.

My confession is not so that I may be forgiven, but because I know I already am. In this quiet prayer time with You, I ask You to help me list out distressing things I've done or others have done to me. As the memories begin to flow and as each one is focused, I ask for Your forgiveness and the power to forgive myself and others.

Thank You for Your total absolution. May I be as generous with others as You have been to me. Help me communicate in words the forgiveness I feel. Today is the day to say, "I forgive you." I will engage in reconciling conversations, phone calls, or letters. Help me not to put it off. I will not use the opportunity to remind people of how much they hurt or troubled me, but will simply assure them of Your forgiveness and love, and mine. I will follow up my words with actions of affirmation and reassurance.

Lord, help me to gather up my hurting memories and unload them to You on a consistent basis. You motivate this desire and are always ready to heal me and enable me to be a healing agent with others. Amen.

The Spirit of the Lord is upon Me, because He has
anointed Me to preach the gospel to the poor;
He has sent Me to heal the brokenhearted...

LUKE 4:18

WHEN I NEED TO GIVE THANKS

Enter into His gates with thanksgiving,
And into His courts with praise.
Be thankful to Him, and bless His name.
For the LORD is good; His mercy is everlasting,
And His truth endures to all generations.

PSALM 100:4-5

Lord, I read the Bible and there it is: the persistently repeated admonition to give thanks. I know You well enough to know that You do not need the assurance of my gratitude. Surely, the need for thanksgiving must have something to do with my spiritual health. The psalmist said, "O LORD my God, I will give thanks to You forever." In this life and in heaven, forever is a long time. Paul said, "In everything give thanks; for this is the will of God for you."

In everything, Lord? Suddenly I know the secret. Thanksgiving is the memory of the heart. I have great memories of Your faithfulness. They become cherished memories as I tell You how grateful I am, not only for Your blessings, but, for You. I say with Joyce Kilmer, "Thank God for God!"

Most important of all, I know that when I thank You for all Your good gifts, the growth of false pride is stunted. And when I can thank You even for the rough and tough things in life, I really can let go of my control and trust You to bring good out of the most distressing things. And so, I give thanks!

I close this prayer of gratitude with special thanks for Christ—His life, message, death, resurrection, and presence. In His majesty and power I pray. Amen. (Psalm 30:12; 1 Thessalonians 5:18.)

It is good to give thanks to the LORD,
And to sing praises to Your name, O Most High;
To declare Your lovingkindness in the morning,
And Your faithfulness every night.

PSALM 92:1-2

WHEN I NEED A SENSE OF
THE VALUE OF TIME

As for me, I trust in You, O LORD;
I say, "You are my God."
My times are in Your hand.

PSALM 31:14-15

Dear God, a thousand years in Your sight are like yesterday when it is past. Lord of Time, You divide my life into years, months, weeks, and hours. As I live my life, You make me very conscious of the passage of time, the shortness of time to accomplish what I want, and my impatience with other people's priorities in the use of time. I've learned that work expands to fill the time available, but also that deadlines are a part of life.

Here I am at the beginning of a crucial day. Grant me an expeditious use of the hours of this day to accomplish what really needs to be done. Grant me an acute sense of the value of time and my accountability to You for using it wisely. I believe there is enough time in today to do what You want done. I press on without pressure, but with promptness to Your timing. You are always on time, in time, to help me in the use of time. Amen.

Just for Today

Lord, for tomorrow and its needs
I do not pray;
Keep me, my God, from stain of sin
Just for today.
Help me to labor earnestly
And duly pray;
Let me be kind in word and deed,
Father, today.
Let me no wrong or idle word
Unthinking say;
Set Thou a seal upon my lips
Through all today...
So for tomorrow and its needs
I do not pray;
Still keep me, guide me, love me, Lord,
Through each day.

SISTER MARY XAVIER (SYBIL F. PARTRIDGE)

WHEN I NEED TO BE COMMITTED

Choose for yourselves this day whom you will serve.

JOSHUA 24:15

Gracious God, You have revealed that commitment is the key to opening the floodgates for the inflow of Your Spirit. Repeatedly, You have responded to my unreserved commitment to You when faced with challenges and problems. You have provided me with clarity of thought and ingenious solutions. Unexpected blessings happen; serendipitous events occur; people respond; and the tangled mess of details is untangled. Amazed, I look back and realize that it was the moment when I gave up, You took over; when I let go, You took hold; when I rested in You, my strength was replenished.

Today, I prayerfully personalize the assurance of the psalmist, "I commit my way to You, Lord. I also trust in You, and You will bring Your plans to pass. I rest in You, and wait patiently for You."

Dear God, You have ordained that there is one decision I must make every day. It is the most crucial decision in the midst of all the other decisions I will be called to make. I hear Elijah's challenge: You have given me the freedom to choose whom I will serve today. I want to renew my decision to serve You as the only Lord of my life. I know that without this decisive intentionality, I will drift into secondary loyalties. You entrust Your strength, gifts of leadership, and vision to those who start each day with a fresh decision to do everything for Your glory and according to Your specific guidance. In the quiet of this moment I make my decision to worship You and commit everything to You. You alone are my Lord and Savior. Amen. (Psalm 37:5,7.)

Commitment, because it is the final thing, is also the principal thing. A Christian is one who is committed to Jesus Christ in every way. Such commitment is the diametrical opposite of cool detachment, and for that reason it is always hazardous. Because commitment includes involvement and consequent risk, it takes courage to care. The involvement always includes actions and not mere opinions.

ELTON TRUEBLOOD

WHEN I NEED DIVINE INSPIRATION

In quietness and confidence shall be your strength.

ISAIAH 30:15

Almighty God, I surrender my life to You, the work of this day, and the challenges I face. You have made relinquishment the condition for receiving Your grace and guidance. I accept the admonition of Proverbs: "Commit your works to the LORD, and your thoughts will be established." I long to be a divinely inspired thinker. When I commit my problems, plans, and projects to You, You instigate thoughts I would not have conceived without your help. Show me how the sublime secret of intellectual inspiration works.

I claim Your presence. I praise You for Your superabundant adequacy to supply my needs spiritually and intellectually. You establish my thinking and energize my work.

Gracious God, thank You for this time in which I can commune with You, renew my convictions, receive fresh courage, and affirm my dedication to serve You. In Your presence I simply can *be*...and know that I am loved. You love me and give me new beginnings each day. Thank You that I can depend on Your guidance for all that is ahead of me this day. Suddenly I realize that this quiet moment has refreshed me. I am replenished with new hope.

Now I can return to my outer world of challenges and opportunities with greater determination. I consecrate the day; You will show the way, and I will receive Your strength without delay. You are my Lord and Savior. Amen. (Proverbs 16:3.)

Lord, what a change within us one short hour
Spent in Thy presence will avail to make!
What heavy burdens from our bosoms take!
What parched grounds refresh as with a shower!
We kneel, and all around us seems to lower;
We rise, and all, the distant and the near,
Stands forth in sunny outline, brave and clear;
We kneel, how weak; we rise, how full of power!
Why, therefore, should we do ourselves this wrong,
Or others—that we are not always strong—
That we are sometimes overborne with care—
That we should ever weak or heartless be,
Anxious or troubled—when with us is prayer,
And joy and strength and courage are with Thee?

RICHARD C. TRENCH

WHEN I NEED CHRIST'S CHARACTER TRAITS FOR MY TRIALS

I am the vine, you are the branches. He who abides in Me, and I in him, bears much fruit; for without Me you can do nothing. If anyone does not abide in Me, he is cast out as a branch and is withered; and they gather them and throw them into the fire, and they are burned. If you abide in Me, and My words abide in you, you will ask what you desire, and it shall be done for you. By this My Father is glorified, that you bear much fruit; so you will be My disciples.

JOHN 15:5-8

Gracious Christ, You have told me that if I, as a branch, am connected to You, the Vine of virtue, my life will emulate Your character. I dedicate this day to live as Your branch for the flow of Your Spirit. I admit that apart from You, I can accomplish nothing of lasting significance. I ask that I may be distinguished with the fruit of Your Spirit, a cluster of divinely inspired, imputed, and induced traits of Your nature reproduced in me.

Your love encourages me and gives me security; Your joy uplifts me and gives me exuberance; Your peace floods my heart with serenity; Your patience calms my agitation over difficult people and pressured schedules; Your kindness enables me to deal with my own and other people's shortcomings; Your goodness challenges me to make a renewed commitment to absolute integrity; Your faithfulness produces trustworthiness that makes me more dependable; Your gentleness reveals the might of true meekness, that humbly draws on Your power; Your Lordship gives me self-control because I have accepted Your control of my life.

You are the mighty God. Live in me, Lord, and manifest in me what You want to express through me. You make me strong for tough times! Amen.

> As the Father loved Me, I also have loved you; abide in My love. If you keep My commandments you will abide in My love, just as I have kept My Father's commandments and abide in His love. These things I have spoken to you, that My joy may remain in you, and that your joy may be full.
>
> JOHN 15:9-11

WHEN THE IDOLS OF MY HEART MUST GO

Everyone...who sets up his idols in his heart, and puts
before him what causes him to stumble into iniquity...I
the LORD will answer him who comes, according to
the multitude of his idols, that I may seize...their heart,
because they are...estranged from Me by their idols.

EZEKIEL 14:4-5

Holy, holy, holy, Lord God Almighty! Heaven and earth are filled with Your glory. Praise and thanksgiving be to You, Lord most high. Ruler of the universe, reign in me. Creator of all, recreate my heart to love You above all else. Provider of limitless blessings, may I never forget that I have been blessed to be a blessing.

I commit my life to You. I surrender the false idols of my heart: pride, position, power, past accomplishments. Without You, I could not breathe a breath, think a thought, or devise a plan. May my only source of security be that I have been called to be both Your friend and Your servant. You are the reason for living, the only One I must please, and the One to whom I am ultimately accountable. With complete trust, I dedicate the work of this day to You.

I hear Your assurance, "Be not afraid, I am with you." I place my hope in Your problem-solving power, Your conflict-resolving presence, and Your anxiety-dissolving peace.

Lord, You have helped me discover the liberating power of an unreserved commitment to You. When I commit my life to You and each of the challenges I face, I am not only released from the tension of living on my own limited resources, but I begin to experience the mysterious movement of Your providence. The company of heaven plus people and circumstances begin to rally to my aid. Unexpected resources are released; unexplainable good things start happening. I claim the promise of Psalm 37: "Commit your way to the LORD, trust also in Him, and He shall bring it to pass." Thank You, dear God, for doing it today! Amen. (Psalm 37:5.)

The dearest idol I have known
Whate'er that idol be
Help me to tear it from Thy throne
And worship only Thee.

WILLIAM COWPER

WHEN ABSOLUTE
HONESTY IS REQUIRED

Put off...the old man...and be renewed in
the spirit of your mind, and...put on the
new man which was created according to
God, in true righteousness and holiness.

EPHESIANS 4:22-24

L ord God of truth, who calls me to absolute honesty
in everything I say, I renew my commitment to truth.
In a time in which people no longer expect to hear the
truth, or what's worse, don't see the need consistently to
speak it, make me a straight arrow who hits the target
of absolute honesty. Help me to be a person on whom
others always can depend for unswerving integrity.

Thank You for keeping me from those little white
lies that later need big black ones to cover them up.
May the reliability of my words earn me the right to
give righteous leadership. Thank You for the wonderful freedom that comes from a consistency between
what I promise and what I do. You are present where
truth is spoken.

Spirit of the living God, fall afresh on me. I need

Your strength. The wells of my own resources run dry. I need Your strength to fill up my diminished reserves—silent strength that flows into me with artesian resourcefulness, quietly filling me with renewed power. You alone can provide strength to think clearly, to decide decisively, and to speak honestly. Amen.

Therefore, putting away lying, "Let each one of you speak truth with his neighbor," for we are members of one another. "Be angry, and do not sin": do not let the sun go down on your wrath, nor give place to the devil. Let him who stole steal no longer, but rather let him labor, working with his hands what is good, that he may have something to give him who has need. Let no corrupt word proceed out of your mouth, but what is good for necessary edification, that it may impart grace to the hearers. And do not grieve the Holy Spirit of God, by whom you were sealed for the day of redemption. Let all bitterness, wrath, anger, clamor, and evil speaking be put away from you, with all malice. And be kind to one another, tenderhearted, forgiving one another, even as God in Christ forgave you.

EPHESIANS 4:25-32

WHEN GOD HIMSELF IS THE ANSWER

God be merciful to us and bless us, and cause
His face to shine upon us, that Your way may be
known on earth, Your salvation among all nations.

PSALM 67:1-2

Dear God, You, Yourself, are the answer to my
prayers. So often I come to You with my long list
of requests. Prayer becomes a "gimme" game rather than
a grace gift. Help me to realize that whatever You give
or withhold from me in prayer is to draw me into deeper
intimacy with You. When I put the primary emphasis
on a relationship with You, experiencing Your presence
and receiving Your power, life becomes a privilege and
loses its strain and stress. Added to that, You provide
the spiritual gifts I need of wisdom and discernment,
emotional strength and stability, and physical stamina
and endurance. Grant me a special measure of Your
inspiration today as I listen to You. Speak to me before
I speak to the people in my life.

In the quiet of this magnificent moment of conversation with You, I dedicate this day. I want to live it to
Your glory, alert to the dangers of this time, but without

anxiety, prepared but not perplexed. I praise You that it is Your desire to give Your presence and blessings to those who ask You. You give strength and power to Your people when we seek You above anything else. You guide the humble and teach them Your way. Help me to humble myself as I live this day so that no self-serving agenda or self-aggrandizing attitude will block Your blessings. You are my Lord and Savior. Amen.

We do most of our living inside us. Our thinking, feeling, and willing are all within. External events press upon us, but they have meaning only by our inward interpretation. We discover that when we are dealing with the troubles of life. The important thing is not what happens to us but what happens *in* us…

If, therefore, we are to be helped in our battle against temptation and in our war with fear and worry, self-ishness, and greed, we must have help within. Not there, but here! Not outside, but inside.

W.E. SANGSTER

WHEN I LONG FOR
FRIENDSHIP WITH CHRIST

No longer do I call you servants, for a servant
does not know what his master is doing; but I
have called you friends, for all things that I have
heard from My Father I have made known to
you. You did not choose Me, but I chose you and
appointed you that you should go and bear fruit,
and that your fruit should remain, that whatever
you ask the Father in My name He may give you.

JOHN 15:15-16

Gracious Lord Jesus, I need to know You as my friend. It is not for some specific blessing I ask, but for the greatest of all blessings, the one from which all others flow. I dare to ask You for a renewal of the wonderful friendship that makes the conversation called prayer a natural give-and-take divine dialogue. In this sacred moment, I open myself to receive this gift of divine companionship with You. Why is it that I am amazed that You know me better than I know myself? Show me what I need to ask of You so You can demonstrate Your generosity once again.

Open my mind so I may see myself and my relationships from Your perspective. Reveal to me Your priorities, Your plan. I spread out before You my problems and perplexities. Help me to listen attentively to the answers You will give. I ask You to be my unseen, but undeniable, friend.

So often I am driven to my knees to seek Your will. Then You lead me to attempt what I could not pull off in my own strength. I discover that courage is Your gift for answered prayer. At the very moment I cry out for help, You open the floodgates of courage and give me that inner resolve that makes me bold and resolute. Thank You, dear Jesus, my friend, for the fresh supply of courage to be unafraid today.

May my communion with You go deeper as the day unfolds. This is the day You have made; I will "rejoice and be glad in it." Amen.

My Best Friend

I want you to meet my best friend. I've known Him for more than 60 years. He's been with me through trials and tragedies, pain and persecution, ups and downs, success and failure. He is the kind of friend who knows all about me and never goes away. He has a special way of helping me to see myself and do something about it. He accepts me the way I am, and yet that very acceptance makes me want to be all that I was meant to be in spite of all the difficulties around me.

He laughs with me over my mistakes and weeps with me in my sorrows. He has been faithful all through life's battles. I have never been left alone when I suffered criticism, hostility, or resistance for doing what love demanded. He is with me when truth triumphs and is always there to absorb the anguish of defeat in a righteous cause. We share a vision, a hope, a dream together...my friend and I. As a matter of fact, He gives me the daring to be true to what I believe regardless of cost.

He meets all the qualifications of a real friend: He loves without limit; He is loyal when others turn away; He listens to my hurts; and He liberates me to grasp life with gusto, regardless of the consequences. I have only one hope: when I come to the end of this portion of heaven and pass on to the next, the one thing people will remember is that I was His friend. My best friend is Jesus Christ!

God's Best for My Life
Lloyd John Ogilvie

Better than your fondest hopes and expectations, God wants to give you His best for your life. This classic bestseller, in a convenient small size, offers 365 devotions that invite you to discover, explore, and enjoy your loving Father each day.

One-Minute Praises and Promises from the Bible
Steve Miller

This beautiful hardcover volume celebrating God's faithfulness and care offers 250 devotions. A great way to fill your mind with assurances of God's goodness...and your heart with praise and hope.

One-Minute Prayers™ for Men Gift Edition

These brief prayers draw you to the feet of Jesus in a simple format ideal for any man ready to develop the discipline of prayer. This handsome, compact volume also makes a great gift for someone who wants to grow in prayer.

Conversation with God
Lloyd John Ogilvie

Dr. Ogilvie clearly and simply explains the many dimensions of prayer and provides a 30-day guide to help you communicate with God in a deeper and more meaningful way than you may have thought possible.

One-Minute Prayers™ for Those Who Hurt

These personal prayers and Scriptures will lead you to rest during a hectic schedule, direct you to God's will during confusing times, and lead you to the Lord's mending touch during broken times.

One-Minute Prayers™ for Women
Gift Edition

You can discover sacred moments of renewal in these prayers gathered from the popular *One-Minute Prayers for Women* and *One-Minute Prayers for Busy Moms*. These brief conversations with God can lead you to peace, grace, and strength for the day.

To read a sample chapter from these or
any other Harvest House books, go to:

www.harvesthousepublishers.com

HARVEST HOUSE PUBLISHERS

EUGENE, OREGON

Most important of all, I know that when I thank You for all Your good gifts, the growth of false pride is stunted. And when I can thank You even for the rough and tough things in life, I really can let go of my control and trust You to bring good out of the most distressing things. And so, I give thanks!

I close this prayer of gratitude with special thanks for Christ—His life, message, death, resurrection, and presence. In His majesty and power I pray. Amen. (Psalm 30:12; 1 Thessalonians 5:18.)

> It is good to give thanks to the LORD,
> And to sing praises to Your name, O Most High;
> To declare Your lovingkindness in the morning,
> And Your faithfulness every night.
>
> **PSALM 92:1-2**

WHEN I NEED TO GIVE THANKS

Enter into His gates with thanksgiving,
And into His courts with praise.
Be thankful to Him, and bless His name.
For the LORD is good; His mercy is everlasting,
And His truth endures to all generations.

PSALM 100:4-5

Lord, I read the Bible and there it is: the persistently repeated admonition to give thanks. I know You well enough to know that You do not need the assurance of my gratitude. Surely, the need for thanksgiving must have something to do with my spiritual health. The psalmist said, "O LORD my God, I will give thanks to You forever." In this life and in heaven, forever is a long time. Paul said, "In everything give thanks; for this is the will of God for you."

In everything, Lord? Suddenly I know the secret. Thanksgiving is the memory of the heart. I have great memories of Your faithfulness. They become cherished memories as I tell You how grateful I am, not only for Your blessings, but, for You. I say with Joyce Kilmer, "Thank God for God!"